Praise for *How to Coach Your Team*

▌▌ We all want to work with exciting, stimulating and successful teams. This easy-to-digest book delivers practical tools and guidance on how to coach your teams and unlock great performance.'
FRANK RICHARDSON, GROUP HR DIRECTOR, SPIRAX SARCO ENGINEERING PLC

▌▌ Ever wished for an extra four hours a day and some super-human powers? This book will offer an alternative to help you deliver it all and even more – with your team!'
TATIANA MATVEEVA, LEADERSHIP DEVELOPMENT DIRECTOR, JAPAN TOBACCO INTERNATIONAL

▌▌ Read this book and bring out the best in your team – it's full of practical tips, examples and activities.'
ANGELA XU, EXECUTIVE VICE PRESIDENT, RECRUITMENT AND EMPLOYEE DEVELOPMENT, HULT INTERNATIONAL BUSINESS SCHOOL

▌▌ Teamwork in a hospital is essential as it improves outcomes and can even help save lives! This book is a 'lifesaver' to everyone out there who wants to run high-performing teams, a must-read!'
NICK FOX, EXECUTIVE DIRECTOR, BMI HEALTHCARE

How to Coach Your Team

Release team potential and hit peak performance

Pam Jones, Viki Holton and Angela Jowitt

PEARSON

Harlow, England • London • New York • Boston • San Francisco • Toronto • Sydney
Auckland • Singapore • Hong Kong • Tokyo • Seoul • Taipei • New Delhi
Cape Town • São Paulo • Mexico City • Madrid • Amsterdam • Munich • Paris • Milan

PEARSON EDUCATION LIMITED

Edinburgh Gate

Harlow CM20 2JE

United Kingdom

Tel: +44 (0)1279 623623

Web: www.pearson.com/uk

First published 2016 (print and electronic)

ISBN: 978-1-292-07796-3 (print)
     978-1-292-07798-7 (PDF)
     978-1-292-07799-4 (ePub)

British Library Cataloguing-in-Publication Data
A catalogue record for the print edition is available from the British Library

Library of Congress Cataloging-in-Publication Data
A catalog record for the print edition is available from the Library of Congress

10 9 8 7 6 5 4 3 2 1
20 19 18 17 16

Cover design: Rob Day
Cover image: Getty Images: nathaphat

Print edition typeset in 9.25/14pt Frutiger LT Com by SPi Global
Print edition printed by Ashford Colour Press Ltd, Gosport

NOTE THAT ANY PAGE CROSS REFERENCES REFER TO THE PRINT EDITION

Contents

Part 3 Pulling it all together: A compact guide for everyday coaching situations 252

About the authors

Pam Jones

Pam has over 20 years' experience designing, developing and delivering leadership programs, and coaching managers. She is Director of open programs at Ashridge Executive Education, Hult International Business School, and professor of practice in academic leadership. She consults internationally with a range of organisations and has worked with HSBC based in Hong Kong and Monash Mount Elisa Business School in Australia.

Pam's passion is helping managers to develop their leadership potential and helping teams to enhance their performance. She has published five books including *Managing for Performance* and *The Performance Management Pocketbook*.

Viki Holton

Viki is Senior Research Fellow at Ashridge Executive Education, Hult International Business School. Over the last 20 years she has been involved in a number of major research projects including women as leaders, diversity, motivation and team development. For a number of years she was a member of the Ashridge Centre for Business and Society and closely involved in the early development of the European Women's Management Development Network.

Viki regularly presents at conferences internationally. Her publications include Ashridge Research Reports such as 'Teams: Succeeding in Complexity', with Pam Jones, and a recent book, *How to Thrive and Survive as a Working Woman: The Coach Yourself Toolkit*.

Angela Jowitt

 Angela is Founder and Director of Dolphin Team Development Ltd, and an Associate Faculty Member at Ashridge Executive Education, Hult International Business School.

For over a decade, Angela has worked extensively with teams from all sectors both nationally and internationally. Her research is in the field of experiential and holistic approaches to learning. Out of this research, she has created a coaching framework which encourages a balanced approach between thinking, feeling and doing.

Angela has published several articles for academic and trade press on the subject of team development, as well as authoring a chapter for a recently published book, *Management Development that Works.*

Publisher's acknowledgements

We are grateful to the following for permission to reproduce copyright material:

Figures

Figure 7.2 adapted from Exhibit from "Alchemy of Growth", 2000, McKinsey & Company, www.mckinsey.com. Copyright © 2015 McKinsey & Company. All rights reserved. Reprinted by permission; Figure 10.1 reprinted with the permission of Scribner, a Division of Simon & Schuster, Inc., from ON DEATH AND DYING by Dr Elisabeth Kübler-Ross. Copyright © 1969 by Elisabeth Kübler-Ross; copyright renewed © 1997 by Elisabeth Kübler-Ross. All rights reserved.

Tables

Table 11.1 adapted from 5 Steps to Creating Employee Engagement, George, M. (2013), Appirio, https://appirio.com/cloud-powered-blog/5-steps-to-creating-employee-engagement

Authors' acknowledgements

We would very much like to extend our thanks to the 30 managers we interviewed who shared their experiences, successes and challenges of working with teams. We have used many of their stories anonymously throughout the book

Lucy Double, Rachel Swaffield and Robina Sutch reviewed our work. Their feedback helped to shape our overall approach and framework.

We are also grateful to all our colleagues at Ashridge who have provided the time, resources and support to enable to us to work on this project.

Finally, we'd like to thank Nicole Eggleton, our acquisitions editor at Pearson, who had a clear vision for the book and encouraged us all the way.

Introduction

This book is a must-read for anyone who is leading teams to deliver results.

How to Coach Your Team will help you to reflect on your own leadership approach and learn how to build a high-performing team.

You may be:

- an established manager wishing to further develop your skills
- an experienced team leader who is already leading a good team
- an experienced project manager looking for new ideas to develop your team
- someone new to management looking for a place to start
- someone who is not directly leading others, but is part of a team environment
- a learning and development or HR professional looking for ways to help teams across the organisation
- a coach wanting to refresh your approach and develop some new ideas and exercises to use with your clients.

This practical 'hands-on' book will help you deliver game-changing results. Even if you have a successful team you will learn how to up your game and move to the next level of performance.

This is the one book you should keep with you throughout your career!

We all know that when a team is working well it is an exciting, stimulating and successful place to be, that is fun to be part of. However when a team is performing badly it can be de-motivating, exhausting and unproductive.

How to Coach Your Team is about the power of coaching as a real business game changer and it will help you and the team to foster:

- greater collaboration
- increased creativity

- effective decision-making
- greater engagement
- improved relationships
- improved teamwork and productivity
- improved motivation and energy
- improved business performance
- improved confidence.

The aim of this book is to help you to become a team coach and to create an environment where team members can coach each other to deliver game-changing performance.

Coaching has been shown to increase productivity by 30%[1] and there are countless studies demonstrating the impact of improved engagement on a whole range of profitability measures, including retention, absenteeism, customer satisfaction and creativity[2], so you could certainly be looking at creating game-changing results for you and your team.

From our own experience in executive coaching, management development and research we know that coaching is something which works across cultures and continents, generations and functions, and is the easiest way to develop great teams and deliver results.

What is team coaching?

As a team leader you not only need to coach individual team members to achieve success, you also need to coach your team so that they can work together effectively to ensure that they achieve more than they would do on their own. You need to develop a spirit of collaboration and support so that as a team you can outperform and achieve success together.

Don't assume that coaching is for remedial or problem situations. Team coaching is definitely about improving performance, 'upping' your game, so your team can excel. Top sports teams will always focus on how to be even more successful. They never stop learning or seeking ways to improve their performance.

There are many different types of team structure. Whether you are working with an established team which is co-located, or a more fluid team brought together for a specific purpose, you will find plenty of ideas to help your team succeed.

There are lots of definitions of coaching but one of the most relevant is from Sir John Whitmore who refers to coaching as 'Unlocking a person's potential to maximize their own performance'[3].

Team coaching goes much further than this. As well as unlocking individual potential, it also focuses on:

- creating a coaching environment where team members collaborate to coach and support each other
- unlocking the potential of the team and bringing together their individual skills and capabilities
- setting and achieving the goals and outcomes with the team
- working together to overcome challenges and deliver innovative solutions.

Our definition of team coaching is *'Engaging in a shared process that is focused on improving performance and developing individual and team capabilities, to achieve game-changing results.'*

What is the difference between individual and team coaching?

There are many similarities between individual and team coaching. Both require excellent skills in listening, questioning and helping people to develop solutions to improve their performance. However, team coaching takes things to a different level. You are not just listening to the individuals in the team, but to the flow of the conversation and the way the team is interacting. You are working with the whole team to develop solutions and build performance. In addition, as a team coach you need to be aware of the wider environment. Teams don't operate in isolation. They are connected and work with a whole range of stakeholders. You need to work with the team to understand how to connect with the wider context both internally and externally.

INDIVIDUAL COACHING	TEAM COACHING
• Works on a one-to-one basis • Helps people to improve their own performance or acquire new skills • Focuses on individual development and solutions • Coaching often takes place 'off the job'	• Works with the whole team • Focuses on improving team dynamics and helping the team understand what they can improve to build performance • Identifies and strengthens the connections between the team and the wider organisation • Creates a model of coaching where members of the team have the ability to coach each other • Coaching sessions often take place in 'real time' when the team is working together

Why team coaching?

There are plenty of books about building and leading teams, so you may well be asking why team coaching, and how can it help you to deliver game-changing results?

Our focus on team coaching is based on 10 years of research, working with managers and teams. As a result we have a good understanding of their challenges and how they have adapted their leadership approach to work with different people and operate effectively in different team structures and environments to achieve success.

We will be drawing on the examples and stories of some of these managers to share their experiences to help bring the contents alive.

There are a number of drivers which have influenced the move towards team coaching as a major aspect of team leadership. These are:

1   the overall complexity of the teams in which we work

2   the environment in which teams are operating

3   the move towards a more collaborative approach to leadership.

Teams are becoming more complex

Working in teams is becoming more complicated and demanding. Look at the diagram below and think about which ones apply to your own team.

Figure 0.1   Team complexities

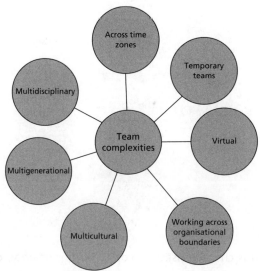

As well as being aware of the structure of your team you also need to understand the individual team members. Different people need different approaches to bring out the best in them. Increasingly, we are working with more multigenerational and multicultural teams. The more complex your team, the more you need to rely on the skills and expertise of others. You simply can't do it all yourself. Team coaching is a way of harnessing the skills of the team and also sharing leadership and responsibility more widely. This is equally important if you are working in a more traditional team format as it will help to grow and develop the team.

The work environment is less predictable

It is not only the world of teams which is getting more complicated, but also the general environment we work and live in.

How many of you are working in a certain, predictable world which stays exactly the same?

Many teams are operating in what is now referred to as the VUCA world[4].

Figure 0.2   The VUCA world

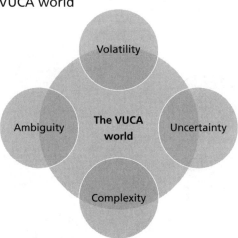

In a world which is characterised by volatility, uncertainty, complexity and ambiguity, problems and issues are not always easy to resolve and require the input and ideas from the whole team.

Working in a more complex and messy world requires a different focus on leadership. The ideas and solutions for the future don't rely on any one individual, but on developing options and approaches with others.

It is not only the external world which has become more complex. Many people are working in environments where they are contributing to a number of different teams with multiple reporting lines. Their success often depends on the contribution and support of different stakeholders. Whilst this can provide a flexible and responsive environment, it can also create constraints and pressures which you need to be aware of.

The role of the team coach is to help build the resilience in the team so that they can manage these complexities and develop ideas and solutions to move forward together.

Changing views of leadership

Traditional leadership approaches have created a sort of superhuman image of what a leader needs to be, and many managers we meet get caught up trying to emulate this. We find that in any leadership session we can often fill a flip chart or two with 'the characteristics of an effective leader'. Yet have you ever met anyone who can do and be everything?!

We believe that there seems to be a shift taking place, not only from a leadership perspective but also from team members. There is an increasing realisation that:

- People want to be involved and will be more enthused and motivated if they have a part in the decision-making process.
- It's OK for leaders not to have all the answers.
- A more collaborative approach will lead to more innovative solutions.
- Leadership is a relational skill, about communicating and building connections.
- Leadership can be shared with the others in the team.

Team coaching is not just about you coaching your team, but creating the environment where team members can coach each other and where the team can coach you as well.

Changing views of leadership

How to use this book

How to Coach Your Team is divided into three parts.

Part one: Team coaching essentials

The essentials of team coaching will provide you with the toolkit to start coaching your team. It focuses on building your skills and ability. You will be able to reflect on your leadership approach and develop your expertise as a team coach. You will also have the opportunity to understand more about your team and the way they work and interact together.

Part two: Achieving game-changing results

This part concentrates on how you can use a team coaching approach in a practical way to deliver game-changing results. There are three important aspects to this:

1   a clear focus on the outcomes you and the team need to achieve
2   a focus on the people in your team, to help them maximise their contribution

Figure 0.3   The focus for achieving game-changing results

3 a focus on communication, the glue that holds the team together and enables you to work and interact effectively.

Using a practical approach with questionnaires, exercises and checklists, you will be able to create your own personal team coaching approach and the tools can be used to build greater collaboration in your team.

Part three: Pulling it all together

Part three pulls all the learning together into a compact guide and reference for everyday coaching challenges and situations. It acts as a pocket guide so that you can apply your coaching skills to work with your team on the most commonly experienced team challenges. It also provides a ready reference for most of the frequently asked questions managers have about putting team coaching into practice. Finally, it equips you with ideas for your own development so that you can continually improve and refresh your skills and expertise.

This is a book which you can work through in a systematic way. It is also a great book to keep as a handy reference throughout your career as a team leader. You can consult the relevant sections as the need arises. For those new to team coaching and team leadership it will help you to build a solid foundation and a resource of ideas and activities you and your team can use. For those who are more experienced in this field it will help you to refresh your approach and take away new insights and ideas. We have focused on providing practical tools and techniques, insights with take-away messages, suggestions and top tips to make your life as team leader easier and, above all, to make your team more effective.

part one

Team coaching essentials

Part one: Team coaching essentials is designed to provide you with the essential skills to coach and develop your team. The starting point for this part is to focus on yourself and reflect on your role as team leader. A team coaching approach is very much about helping team members to come up with solutions, and develop the confidence to work together. Your role therefore requires you to be a facilitator and catalyst, bringing out the best in others.

In Chapter 2 you will have the opportunity to develop and enhance your coaching skills. Team coaching is similar to individual coaching; the main difference however, is that you are working with the team. Not only do you have the complexity of working with the whole team, but you are also working on real-time issues that your team is facing. Don't be daunted. Once you have mastered the basic skills of coaching you can start to adapt them to working with your team.

Figure 0.4   Team coaching essentials

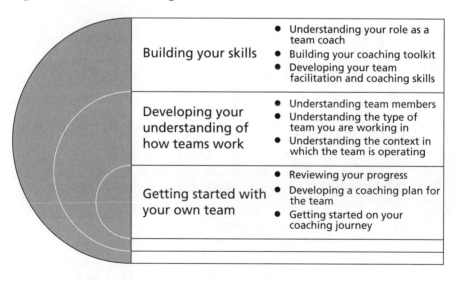

An important aspect of team coaching is developing an understanding of how teams work. Each of your team members will have different personalities, strengths and skills. A high-performing team will need to work together effectively to maximise their full potential. Understanding more about team dynamics and facilitation will help you and the team function more effectively.

Finally, as a team coach you need to be aware of the context in which you are working. All teams are different and you need to adapt your approach to the type of team you are working with and the organisational context in which you are operating.

The techniques and skills discussed in this part will provide you with a toolkit which you can develop and hone as you step out on your journey as a team coach. At the end of Part one you will have the opportunity to review your progress and create a practical coaching plan for you and your team.

Your role

It's not often that we take a step back and think about our role as a leader. This chapter offers you a chance to do just that and take the opportunity to fine tune or change the way you work in order to develop your role as a team coach.

In this chapter you will have the opportunity to:

- understand your role as a team coach
- develop a coaching mindset
- develop your team coaching approach.

How do you see your role?

Look at the statements on the following two pages and indicate where your preference is for leading your team. Try to be honest and think about examples from your day-to-day work.

	STRONGLY AGREE	AGREE	NEUTRAL	AGREE	STRONGLY AGREE	
As a team leader I am responsible for making all the decisions						Decision-making involves the team and I trust team members to make the best decision
I like to be in control of what is hap-pening in the team						I am happy for team members to take control
I have a strong task focus and drive results						I have a strong focus on building the relation-ships in the team
Leadership in the team is my responsibility						Leadership can be shared with and in the team
I am some-times reluctant to delegate as I feel the work may not be up to my standard						I delegate tasks to team members as a way of devel-oping their skills and competence
I just don't have time to coach my people						I see coaching and develop-ing the team as a core aspect of my role

▶

	STRONGLY AGREE	AGREE	NEUTRAL	AGREE	STRONGLY AGREE	
I often have the answer and know what needs to happen						I am always keen to listen to team members and encourage them to come up with the solution

If you scored mostly towards the left-hand side of the page you are a very dedicated team leader who has a clear focus on the task and a strong sense of responsibility. Your more directional approach may be appropriate in certain situations, but it is not a style that will develop and bring out the best in others. This approach may also result in long working hours and may prevent you from operating strategically, as your focus will be on controlling and managing the situation.

If you want to become more of a team coach then reflect on the statements on the right-hand side of the questionnaire. Team coaching is a style of leadership which is about facilitating the development of the team. It is about collaborating and working with the team and external stakeholders to achieve the goal. It is much more suited to our current, complex world of work. In addition, it is an approach which will not only bring out the best in others, but will also help you to achieve a greater degree of work-life balance.

However, this approach also requires you to 'let go' and recognise that you don't know all the answers. It needs you to be curious and genuinely interested in any new approaches and ideas your team suggests.

Ideally your leadership approach should vary and change depending on the situation and the people you are working with. It is well worth reflecting on this and thinking about any changes and adjustments you need to make.

You may need to be more directive when you are giving instructions, passing on information or setting expectations. However, if you want to explore ideas, think of different approaches and involve others it is important to adopt a more facilitative approach.

Getting this balance isn't always easy, as one leader told us: 'There are times when it's really important to be directive, and others when you need to step back. The challenge is knowing when. It's important to ensure that you don't just fall back on your default style.'

Figure 1.1 Getting the balance right for team coaching

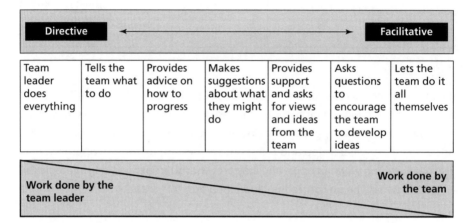

Try this

In your next team meeting make sure you build in time to involve the team in thinking about some of the key decisions. Listen carefully and encourage an open discussion, where everyone can be involved. Summarise the discussion at the end and agree how you will all move ahead.

Developing your emotional intelligence

Emotional intelligence is the capacity to tune in to other people's emotions, so that you can understand them. This helps to build a better appreciation of the situation and to take appropriate action.

Hay Group identified four elements which make up emotional intelligence[1]. These are:

Self-awareness	Your ability to understand yourself, to have a good self-assessment of your own style, motives and impact on others.
Self-management	Your ability to manage your emotions and reactions and adapt to different situations.
Social awareness	Your ability to read and understand others, to show empathy and build rapport. This also applies to understanding your customers and the organisation.
Relationship management	Your ability to manage relationships with others through team building, influencing and conflict management.

Figure 1.2 Emotional intelligence

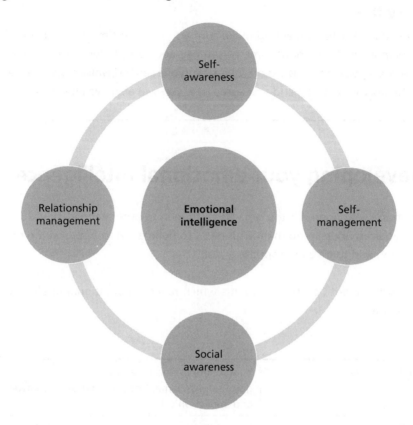

Emotional intelligence is at the heart of becoming a team coach. Looking at the descriptions you can probably identify areas where you are more skilled than others. We have provided some ideas, suggestions and top tips to help you on your team coaching journey (see Table 1.1).

Table 1.1 Suggestions to improve your emotional intelligence

COMPONENTS OF EMOTIONAL INTELLIGENCE	DEVELOPMENT IDEAS
Self-awareness	• Gain feedback from others about your approach. • Reflect on the Head, Heart and Gut questionnaire in Chapter 4 to gain an understanding of your style. • Monitor your emotions and think about how you come across to others. • Be clear about your personal values and goals.

▶

COMPONENTS OF EMOTIONAL INTELLIGENCE	DEVELOPMENT IDEAS
Self-management	• Practise observing and noticing how you feel and ask yourself why you feel this way. • Take responsibility for your feelings and behaviour. • Take some time for reflection before you react. Don't let tempers flare. • Manage your stress levels as under stress we often behave inappropriately.
Social awareness	• Take time to listen to others. • Understand the needs of your stakeholders. • Understand your team, who they are, and what motivates them. • Empathise with others and try to see things from their perspective.
Relationship management	• Create a positive environment in your team which encourages collaboration. • Plan how to influence and work effectively with your stakeholders. • Take a positive approach to managing change. • Take time to build relationships both within and outside the team.

We will be covering many of these areas as you work through this book so make a note of your strengths and development areas and take time to complete the questionnaires and activities in the relevant chapters.

As a team coach you also need to identify opportunities to develop others. One of the ways of achieving this is to look at your own workload and the projects and activities that could be delegated to others.

Looking for opportunities to coach: the coaching delegation link

Figure 1.3 Combining delegation and coaching

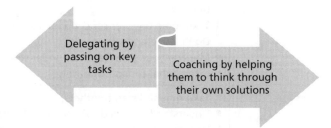

Coaching and delegation can go hand in hand. It's a great way to develop your team and to manage your workload.

We often think of delegation as literally passing on work to someone else. However, if it's done effectively it can help to:

- develop the skills in the team
- build confidence in others
- motivate and empower others
- lead to new and better solutions
- ease your workload.

WHY MANAGERS DON'T DELEGATE

Figure 1.4 Reasons why managers don't delegate

If you don't delegate, it's worth thinking about why and questioning your assumptions. It's never quicker to do the job yourself in the long run and as one manager said: 'If someone can do 80% of the job I'll delegate it to them and coach the rest.' So:

- Look at your team. What skills do they need to develop? What tasks could you pass on which would help their development?
- Look at your own job and make sure you delegate tasks that are developmental for someone else.

Figure 1.5 Combining delegation and coaching

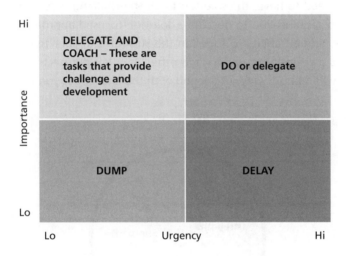

Use Figure 1.5 to think about some tasks you could delegate which fit into the top left-hand box. This is the important-but-not-yet-urgent box so you have time to delegate and coach someone to work on this knowing that it will stretch them and provide learning. The more planning you can do, the easier it will be to delegate and coach tasks before they get into the high importance and high urgency box, when you just may not have the time to pass it on to others.

When you are linking delegation to coaching:

- Link the task to the interest and development of your team members.
- Explain the outcome of the task and the key deliverables but ask them how they think they could proceed.
- Find out what help they need and whether anyone else in the team can provide this.
- Fix times when you can check in and review the progress.

- Provide feedback on what is working well and what could be improved.

- Help to provide access to data and resources which they may need to complete the task.

- Remember to give credit to the team member and at the end review the process and the learning they have gained.

Developing a coaching mindset

Developing a coaching mindset involves recognising that you don't have, and don't need to have, the solution to all the challenges you and the team face. It also requires you to develop a solution-focused approach to meeting challenges, and an ability to focus on the strengths in your team. Combined with this is a curiosity to understand other people's perspectives in order to create new and better ways of dealing with the challenges you face.

Figure 1.6 The coaching mindset

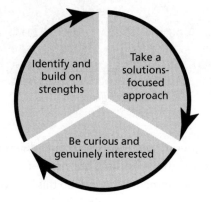

FOCUS ON SOLUTIONS

Many of us like to be regarded as good problem solvers. From school onwards we have learned to analyse situations, looking at what's wrong, and come up with a solution. Yet in a coaching situation this is not always effective.

One of the coaching exercises we often use is to ask people to focus on a problem they are currently experiencing. The coach asks the following questions:

- How long has this been going on?

- Why did it happen?

- Why hasn't it been solved?
- Who is to blame?
- What are you going to do to put it right?

They then repeat the exercise with a different and more positive set of questions:

- What is it you want to achieve?
- What is working well?
- What can you build on to improve the situation?
- Who can help you?
- How can you move forward?

There is no prize for guessing which set of questions is the most helpful. The first set of questions is focused on the cause of the problem. This may be appropriate for solving technical problems but these questions can often drag down motivation and end up creating a blame cycle.

The second set of questions is more concerned with moving towards a solution. Focusing on solutions assumes that there is a better way, that people are resourceful in coming up with ideas, and that small changes can help to move things forward. People usually feel more energised and creative when you take a solution-focused approach.

Insight

It can take time when you want team members to take greater responsibility, as the following example illustrates:

We were all working on a key project and one of my guys came back to tell me that a technical task was not possible. I was pretty sure it was, but rather than take over I asked him how he'd reached this decision and encouraged him to go back to the data again. He was able to identify a solution and in the process build his technical knowledge.

TAKE AWAY

You don't always have to give the answer. Be positive and encourage people to find solutions for themselves.

Build on strengths

In the same way as we are encouraging you to take a more solution-focused approach, it is also important to focus on the strengths of the team and explore how you and the team can work with and build on these strengths.

Strengths have been defined as 'the underlying qualities that energise us, contribute to our personal growth and lead to peak performance'[2].

People who are working with their strengths are likely to be more productive, resilient and confident. We all love doing things we are successful at, and playing to strengths has been shown to increase productivity, creativity and engagement in the workplace.

It is important that people are aware of their strengths and how they contribute to the team. They also need to be aware of any possible challenges that can be caused by over-using the strengths. For example, someone who is helpful and supportive of others can end up not doing their own work. Someone who is energetic and task focused can end up being single-minded and directive if they overuse that strength.

Insight

One management team we worked with was struggling because the four team members had very different strengths. Two members of the team were very commercially driven and entrepreneurial, another more thoughtful and analytical, and the fourth member of the team was more concerned with relationships and supporting people. There was a lot of tension in the team, especially as under stress they tended to overuse their key strengths. However,

▶

once the team started to understand each other and the strengths they brought to the team, they started to listen to each other and work together more effectively. The two action-oriented commercial people started to analyse some of the risks they were thinking of taking and also take into account the effect on the people in the organisation. The more thoughtful person also recognised the need to take risks and try things out. The fourth team member learned to enter the debate, have an opinion and not worry if this might not please everyone. Being more objective made this much easier. Everyone had to step outside their comfort zone and adapt their style.

TAKE AWAY

Understand, discuss and use the strengths in the team.

This Insight has highlighted three personality strengths which the team members demonstrated: two had a focus on action, another on detail and the fourth team member on relationships.

Figure 1.7 Working with strengths

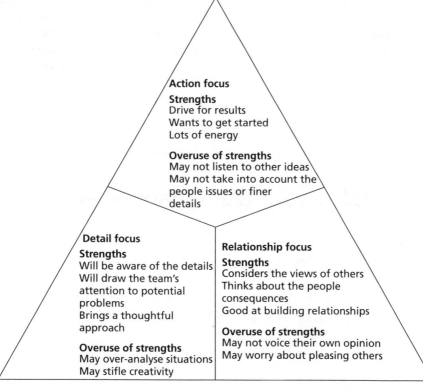

Action focus
Strengths
Drive for results
Wants to get started
Lots of energy

Overuse of strengths
May not listen to other ideas
May not take into account the people issues or finer details

Detail focus
Strengths
Will be aware of the details
Will draw the team's attention to potential problems
Brings a thoughtful approach

Overuse of strengths
May over-analyse situations
May stifle creativity

Relationship focus
Strengths
Considers the views of others
Thinks about the people consequences
Good at building relationships

Overuse of strengths
May not voice their own opinion
May worry about pleasing others

There are many other strengths that people demonstrate associated with their technical skills or other characteristics, such as creativity, networking or logical thinking, just to name a few.

As you work through Part one you will have the opportunity to use some questionnaires and exercises to help the team build an understanding of their overall team strengths. Remember this is something you can do together as a way of getting to understand each other.

Try this

Reflect on your team. What are the strengths of each team member? Are any of the team overusing their strengths? Identify your own strengths and how you use them. Finally, think about how you can work as a team to make the most of each other's strengths as you move forward.

Use this table to think about your existing strengths and those of your team.

Add in the names of your team members	Strengths	How can you build on these strengths?	How can you recognise and manage any overused strengths?
You			

Developing your team coaching approach

Developing as an individual and team coach requires you to reflect on your own leadership approach and the assumptions you hold about working with others.

Coaching is not just something you do during a 'coaching meeting.' It is a central part of your leadership approach and should inform every conversation or interaction you have with your team.

Top tips

- Be curious and explore other people's ideas and perspectives.
- Stand back from always suggesting an answer and ask questions so that you are a catalyst for new ideas.
- Focus on outcomes and how to move forward.
- Work with the team to recognise and build on each other's strengths.
- Your role is to build the team's confidence so that they have faith in their own ability to succeed.

Summary

A team coaching approach requires you to genuinely want to get the best out of the team by helping them to develop the confidence and ability to come up with ideas and take greater responsibility for creating solutions and achieving success.

We have explored some of the attitudes and mindset changes required by a team coach and have encouraged you to reflect on your role.

Identify a couple of small changes you could make to build on your strengths and develop your coaching approach, and monitor the progress and results you make over the next few months.

Actions from this chapter

ACTION	TIME FRAME	TEAM INVOLVEMENT	REFLECTIONS AND PROGRESS REVIEW
1.			
2.			
3.			

There is an example of a completed action plan on the next page.

Completed Action Plan

ACTION	TIME FRAME	TEAM INVOLVEMENT	REFLECTIONS AND PROGRESS REVIEW
1. Take the opportunity to LISTEN more to team members	Over the next month/ongoing	I need to spend some quality time with each of the team.	I've noticed that I'm finding out more about the team members and they seem to be more confident in expressing their ideas.
2. Identify some delegation/ coaching opportunities for the team	Over the next month	I've delegated a couple of projects to the team and paired up people to work on them together. We have weekly review meetings to check progress.	This seems to be going well and I'm getting positive feedback from the team and some great results.
3. Identify and work with team strengths	Over the next month	I've started to think more about how to work with the strengths in the team and one success has been asking one of the team members who is more people focused to plan and organise our next team event.	The team event was really successful and energising. I need to do this more!

Developing your skills

This chapter will focus on the four building blocks important for coaching others in a team context. Gallup research shows that the people skills of a leader can add 25% to business returns and contribute up to 70% to the organisational climate so it's well worth honing and developing your team coaching toolkit in order to bring out the best in others.

This chapter will help you to:

- develop the four key building blocks for effective coaching
- understand how to use these skills to build performance and motivation in the team
- be able to use these skills with your team.

The four building blocks for effective coaching are: listening, questioning, building rapport, and feedback. These skills are central to one-to-one coaching. However, the difference with team coaching is that you are working with a group of people, often at the same time, so you need to be aware of how to use these skills in a team context.

Figure 2.1 Building blocks for successful coaching

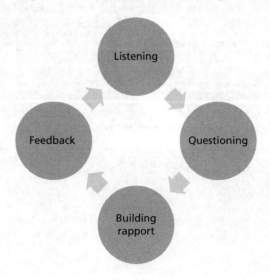

Listening

This is probably the most important skill for any team coach. It will help you to understand the team and the issues they face. If you are listening to others it also demonstrates respect and encourages others to open up and share their concerns and ideas.

> *Listening is such a simple act. It requires us to be present, and that takes practice, but we don't have to do anything else. We don't have to advise, or coach, or sound wise. We just have to be willing to sit there and listen.*[1]

We live in a world that often prevents us from really listening to others, so beware of some things which may stop you listening to others:

- multi-tasking – doing emails and listening at the same time doesn't work!
- letting your mind drift to other issues
- not picking up on changes in body language
- lack of interest
- developing your own solutions and ideas rather than listening to others
- being too rushed and busy
- being selective about what you want to hear.

It really is important to show good active listening when you work as a team coach. This means:

- maintaining good eye contact
- being aware of body language and non-verbal communication
- listening to the flow of conversation in the team
- cultivating empathy and trying to see things from the perspective of others
- refraining from evaluating what is being said
- letting people finish what they have to say
- providing positive feedback and encouragement to show you are listening
- summarising what has been said using their words, getting agreement that you've understood completely
- being aware of your own emotional response to what you are hearing, as this will affect how well you understand and can respond.

If you are really listening effectively you will be listening at three different levels so that you can pick up not only on the **Words** that are spoken but also the **Emotions** and **Energy** level in the team. We refer to this as the **WEE** model for effective listening.

Figure 2.2 The WEE model for effective listening

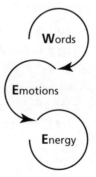

Listening at the level of emotions and energy is very important. If the team, or individuals in the team, are not engaged they will not be committed to moving ahead. The **WEE model** on the next page will help you listen more effectively to others.

Words	Listen to the content and facts in the conversation: • What is being said? • How is the story developing? • Are there differing views? • Who is talking most/least? • There may also be topics/issues that are not being discussed.
Emotions	Listen to the emotions and feelings being expressed by the group by noticing: • Any changes in body language in team members – these can indicate the level of engagement. • The pace of the conversation – is it fast and animated or more reflective? • The facial expressions of team members.
Energy	Listen to the energy and commitment in the team: • Is the language action-focused and positive, or is the team focusing on the problems and difficulties? • Is the team generating and building on ideas, or criticising and putting down suggestions? • Are all the team members involved and are all views being heard?

Insight

One experienced team manager describes a very broad-brush approach to managing people in her team:

I often ring people for a chat when there aren't any business issues. I find this is really helpful in building good relationships. I've also trained myself over the years to listen to both what people are saying and simultaneously think about what's missing; what it might be that they don't say. This often gives me a good steer on any potential problems or topics that people maybe feel that for whatever reason they should not mention to me.

TAKE AWAY

Try to develop your listening skills and tune in to people's emotions.

Try this

Next time you are with your team, try to really listen to what is going on. Clear your mind, and listen to the flow of the conversation and to the emotions and energy in the group. Make sure you summarise on a regular basis and if you are noticing anything in the group then take the opportunity to reflect this back to the team.

Questioning

An important element of coaching is being curious. This requires you to be genuinely interested in the ideas of your team members. It means wanting to understand their perspective, their thinking process and the contribution they want to make. Your role as a coach is also to empower your team to make decisions, work in collaboration and develop innovative ideas. The best way to do this is to hold back from telling people what to do. Instead ask good-quality, open questions such as: 'How can we move things forward?' 'Who should we be working with?' 'What do you think are the next steps?'.

Often managers, when they are starting to coach, fall in to the trap of asking closed questions such as: 'Have you thought about doing x?' This is really an instruction in disguise.

The questions you ask as a coach should be very much aimed at helping the other person or the team develop their awareness, their ideas and their sense of responsibility to move forward.

Good questions help to:

- build confidence in the team and individual team members
- empower the team to make informed decisions
- share information and ideas
- explore the diversity of views in the group
- build trust and respect
- encourage the team to develop
- create new approaches and innovations.

Remember that the questions you ask when you are coaching will either limit or expand the responses you get.

Here is a list of ten great coaching questions you can use with others. These are all open questions which will help the other person take responsibility and come up with new ideas and develop the commitment and motivation to move ahead.

Ten great coaching questions

1 What do you want to achieve?

2 How will you know when you have done a great job?

3 What have you done so far?

4 What else do you need to do?

5 What is holding you back?

6 What have you learned?

7 What support do you need?

8 Who can help you?

9 How can you get started?

10 What is the first step you can take?

Building rapport

Rapport is central to building effective relationships. The dictionary definition of rapport is:

> *A close and harmonious relationship in which the people or groups concerned understand each other's feelings or ideas and communicate well.*

It occurs naturally when we have a positive and trusting relationship with others, and in turn this helps to build trust and develop more positive communication patterns.

Rapport is made up of three basic elements: the content of the conversation, body language and the energy and pace expressed.

Figure 2.3 The three elements of good rapport

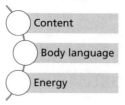

If you do a bit of people watching, rapport is easy to observe in others as their body language will naturally be in sync with the person they are talking to. They will be sitting in the same way, for example leaning in at various points in the conversation. This is often referred to as 'mirroring'[2].

CONTENT

We often have rapport regarding the content of what we say, if it is of interest to the other person, and if we are in agreement. The challenge is to maintain rapport when we disagree with others. One way to achieve this is to ensure that you maintain rapport in your body language and energy. By doing this you have more chance of having a healthy discussion rather than an open conflict.

BODY LANGUAGE

Another element of rapport is body language. It's always useful to be aware of your own body language and notice how you use it. For example, if you want to create an open, friendly atmosphere make sure that your body language conveys this, with good eye contact, a smile and open rather than folded arms. Our body language leaks out so much about our feelings and concerns, so make sure you are using it to deliver the messages you want to convey.

As a team coach it's important to reflect on your rapport, and also to reflect on the team, and the rapport they have with each other. This will provide you with information about the team and how they are working together.

ENERGY

Energy literally refers to the level of energy we project. Some people are very fast paced. They talk quickly, varying their voice tone, and have animated hand actions. Others are much slower paced in how they come across, speaking in a more measured, level way with less variation in their voice tone and actions. If you are working virtually with people, content and energy are your main ways of achieving rapport, so you need to really focus on your listening and pick up on the tone, pace and intonation.

MATCHING AND PACING

One of the secrets of creating rapport is to initially match the style of the other person or the team. It's no use bounding in full of enthusiasm if the team is feeling despondent. You must first meet them at their level and then work to lift the energy by gradually increasing your own energy to take them to a different place.

Insight

A manager from an international, virtual team described her approach to building rapport:

> I am always happy to listen to what the team want to tell me. When I'm on a conference call I never multi-task and just focus on what is being said and how it's being said. As I lead a virtual team I have to think about the environment I want to create. I always build in a bit of social time at the beginning of our call, asking people to say what's happening for them, and I always try to make sure that my emails are supportive and friendly. I have noticed that the team responds well to this and we are starting to create a collaborative team culture even though we rarely meet up.

TAKE AWAY

It's helpful for the team to feel that you are genuinely interested in hearing their issues.

Try this

- Do some people watching and observe rapport in others.
- Be aware of how you manage your own rapport. Reflect on your body language and energy. Does it match that of the team and the different members? Think about the type of energy you want to create in the team and how you can adapt your approach to achieve this.

▶

- Ask for feedback on your style and approach. How do you come over to others? What works and how could you improve?

FEEDBACK

Feedback is a real cornerstone of team coaching. It is not just about you giving feedback to the team, but also about creating an environment where the team are comfortable giving feedback to each other and also giving feedback to you.

Try this

Looking back over the last month, think about the feedback you have given to each team member and assess how much of this has been positive, compared to how much has been critical. It's important to have a balance between positive and negative comments and research shows that workgroups with at least a ratio of 3:1 of positive to negative interactions are more productive than those having less than a 3:1 ratio[3].

Figure 2.4 Balancing the ratio of positive to negative interactions

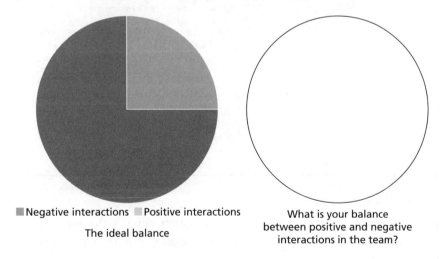

■ Negative interactions ■ Positive interactions

The ideal balance

What is your balance between positive and negative interactions in the team?

The SOFA model of feedback is a useful model for both positive and developmental feedback and it may help you to create a better working environment. The model focuses on four important elements of feedback and provides a framework for preparing any feedback conversation you may need to have with the team and team members.

S	Situation	Describe the situation, by providing some context and talking specifically about the behaviours which are causing concern.
O	Outcomes	Describe the consequences of the behaviour. How does it impact on you and others?
F	Feelings	Describe how it makes you feel. This has a number of advantages in that it labels how you feel in a calm way, and describes the impact of the behaviour on you, which cannot be disputed.
A	Action	It is always important to agree some actions and a way forward. This may be in terms of coaching, setting improvement objectives and agreeing a time to follow up and review the changes.

Figure 2.5 The SOFA model of feedback

Try this

- Next time you have a feedback conversation, either with your team or individuals in the team, use the SOFA model to plan the conversation.

- Think about the ratio of positive to negative feedback you use with your team and rather than saying generalised statements such as 'good job' or 'well done', use the SOFA feedback to be clear about what people did which produced the positive result.

Top tips

- Always clear your mind and listen 100% to others.
- Spend time building rapport as this builds trust in the team.
- Don't jump in with a solution.
- Ask questions to help people think through their ideas.
- Make sure you give plenty of feedback and encouragement but don't avoid the tough issues.

Summary

It is well worth developing and using the four building blocks of listening, questioning, rapport and feedback.

- Rate your performance in the four skills. Which ones do you do well and which ones could you develop further?
- Try some of the ideas mentioned in this chapter and review your progress. What worked? What differences did you notice in yourself and others?
- By building these skills into your everyday leadership practice you will be building your coaching skills and the effectiveness of your team.

Actions from this chapter

ACTION	TIME FRAME	TEAM INVOLVEMENT	REFLECTIONS AND PROGRESS REVIEW
1.			
2.			
3.			

Coaching your team

The focus of this chapter is to bring together the essential skills of coaching in a team setting so that you can actively facilitate meetings, conference calls and team workshops. We then take the final step of introducing the TOPIC framework for team coaching, a process you and your team can learn to use together.

This chapter will help you to:

- develop the skills and ability to facilitate team meetings
- understand the behaviours which help and hinder team performance
- understand and use the TOPIC model of team coaching with your team.

Developing your facilitation skills

Good facilitation skills are essential for any team coach to bring out the best in the team and help to develop involvement and collaboration.

This is probably one of the hardest roles for any team leader or team coach, as it requires balancing a concern for the task, a concern for the process and way the team is working and also a concern for the relationships within the team.

Often when we work with teams, our experience is that they focus mainly on the task, without thinking about how they organise themselves or how they manage the relationships within the teams. This often leads to confusion, wasted time and disagreement on how to move forward.

Figure 3.1 Getting the balance right

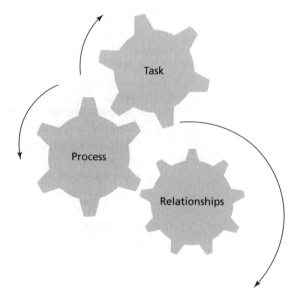

- **The task activities** (see Figure 3.1) cover *what* the team needs to achieve; the outcomes and deliverables.
- **The process activities** are concerned with *how* the team achieves the task. This will involve thinking about the organisation of the team, who does what and how time is allocated.
- **The relationship activities** are concerned with *whom* you are working with. This focuses on the relationships within the team, how team members interact and how they work together to achieve a result.

Before you organise any team meeting or event use the checklist on the next page to make sure you have given sufficient attention to the task, process and relationships in the team.

Attention to the task	What do you and the team need to achieve? Be clear about the outcomes and key success factors for the meeting. Who needs to be at the event? What resources do you need? When do you need to deliver the final results?
Attention to the process	The process element can be split into three sections: before, during and after the event. **Before:** • Set up the venue and logistics • Send out a clear agenda and any preparation required • Plan the event – exercises, speakers, breakouts, etc. **During:** • Manage the time and energy • Identify roles and responsibilities • Manage the decision-making process and minutes of the meeting • Manage the communication flow • Review what went well and what could be improved **Afterwards:** • Follow up – minutes, actions, responsibilities and next steps.
Attention to the relationships	Is everyone involved? Are all ideas being heard? Is everyone listening to each other? Is conflict being managed well? Is everyone on board?

Probably one of the most difficult areas in facilitation is working with the relationships in the team and creating an environment where everyone is involved and contributing to the discussions

On the next page are some of the behaviours you can use to help to create a positive climate in the team[1]. These are shown in Figure 3.2.

POSITIVE TEAM BEHAVIOURS

Figure 3.2 Positive team behaviours

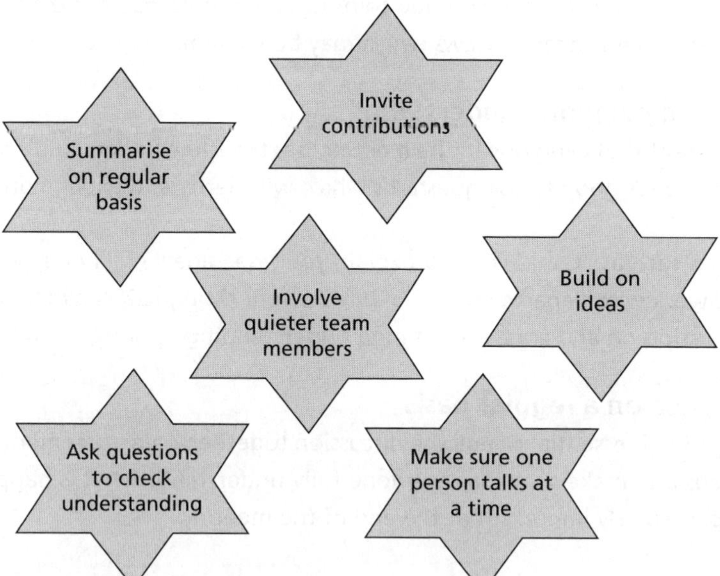

Ask for contributions and ideas

Asking for ideas from the team is a useful way of bringing out a range of suggestions. Ask each person for their ideas so that these can then be evaluated and discussed. This also avoids the issue of people just proposing an idea they are passionate about without considering all the other options.

Build on contributions

Look for ways to develop and build on ideas. For example:

- 'That's interesting, what else could we do to take this forward?'
- 'Jon's idea is interesting. We could think about how it links with what you are doing in your area.'

Support others

You can support others through positive comments and feedback and through your body language by listening attentively and not interrupting.

Include quieter members of the team

People may be quiet in a meeting, but it doesn't mean that they don't have anything to say. Often they may feel under-confident, or in an international setting they may find it hard to contribute when they have to speak in a different language. It's always good to bring quieter members in early on and check if they have ideas or views which may be valuable.

Make sure everyone understands

It's important that everyone in the meeting has the same understanding about the issue, so it's good to ask questions which will clarify and expand on ideas.

Questions such as, 'Could you just explain your idea again?', 'I'm not sure how this will work with department x . . . what are your thoughts?' can help to move the discussion on and create a common understanding.

Summarise on a regular basis

Summarising is essential to pull the discussion together, gain agreement on the next steps and make sure that everyone fully understands what is happening. This is particularly important at the end of the meeting.

As well as noticing and promoting positive behaviours in the team, it is also important to try to avoid some of the behaviours which if overused can have a negative impact on the team. These are shown in Figure 3.3.

BEHAVIOURS TO KEEP IN CHECK

Figure 3.3 Negative team behaviours

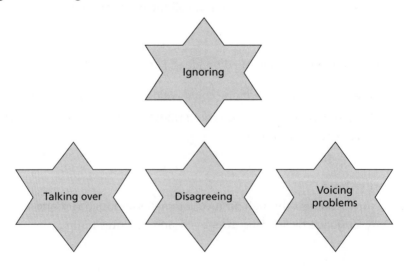

Talking over

Talking over someone else is often a sign of an enthusiastic and passionate team. However it will mean that voices are not heard, ideas are lost and the loudest voice often wins out. As a facilitator you will need to point this out and agree a process where only one person talks at a time.

Ignoring

This is linked to talking over and refers to times when one person is constantly dominating the conversation. They may also be ignoring and cutting out other people in the team. It's important for you to politely bring in the rest of the team. You may even need to have a quiet word with the individual during a break as often they are not aware of their behaviour.

Disagreeing

Whilst disagreement is not a negative behaviour in itself, if it is overused it will be a real barrier to exploring ideas and coming up with creative solutions. One of the most common forms of disagreement is to say: 'Yes . . . BUT we can't do this because of . . . '. If this is happening in your team try to encourage the team to try using: 'Yes AND . . . we will also need to think of . . . '. 'Yes AND . . . ' gives the option of building on what is good in the idea rather than immediately putting it down.

Voicing problems

Again, whilst it is good to identify potential difficulties, if the team is always doing this it can lead to negative thinking and create despondency. Trying to keep a solutions-focused approach will help. For example, it's much better to say 'What can we do to overcome x's views?' than to say 'x will never agree to this'.

Power dynamics

Power is the ability to influence the behaviour of others. People can use power in a negative sense, for their own ends, or equally they can use their power to help others and to work towards a positive outcome.

One thing to be aware of when facilitating and coaching teams is the power differentials which may exist. How do people in the team perceive you as team leader? If they feel afraid or think they are being judged they may not speak out, or will perhaps only say what they think you want to hear.

Coaching is ultimately a relational skill and it's important that the relationship is one where your team can feel comfortable contributing, so try to put the team at ease and explain that you want to hear their views and ideas.

You may also want to think about how the people in the team perceive each other. Some may feel more powerful because of their expertise or experience and this may affect the balance of the discussion in the team. If you are working in a global team there may be perceived power differentials because of people's location or language ability and this may affect the contribution level in the team. On top of this are the power differentials which come from other areas of diversity such as culture, gender, ethnicity and background.

Think about the power dynamics in your team.

- How are you perceived by others?
- How can you ensure the team members who feel less powerful can have a voice?

Power is something which is rarely discussed in organisations but has a huge impact on the way teams operate.

Here are some suggestions to help you manage the power dynamics in your team:

- Build a good relationship in the team so that they can feel comfortable expressing their ideas.
- Have a clear sense of purpose and outcome so you can pull people back to the overall goal.
- Build in opportunities for the team to understand and appreciate what they contribute and the constraints they are working with.
- Try to make sure everyone has a voice in the meeting, by providing opportunities for those who feel less powerful to have a say. This might be by bringing them into the discussion, or encouraging them to prepare something for the meeting.
- You will also need to manage the more dominant team members by controlling the discussion and splitting up any cliques.
- Think about how you set up your meetings – off-site, relaxed meetings in a less formal environment can help to break power differentials down.

Insight

One general manager we worked with planned a strategy meeting for his management team. This was a one-day event. Not only did he need to inform the management team about the new strategy which was being implemented globally, he also needed their buy-in and support for it. He organised an 'off-site' meeting in a relaxed environment and spent time thinking about the room layout so that he could encourage open communication. He opted for working in an open-plan environment rather than the traditional boardroom style. He also set the day up so that people could work in different groups to discuss ideas and issues and then present them back. In this way all the ideas were shared in a creative and productive environment. The day was a success and the team went away feeling confident and supportive of the new approach.

TAKE AWAY

Planning ahead for the style of a meeting, and how discussions are encouraged, will help you get the best from all team members.

Try this

Take some time to plan your next team event. You can get the team to help you. Think about what you want to achieve, what climate you want to create in the team, and use the Task/Process/Relationship model to plan the event. Try to avoid the traditional 'death by PowerPoint' and design an event which creates involvement and commitment. It's often helpful to go off-site or find a place free from interruptions.

Some dos and don'ts for team facilitation

There are some helpful suggestions about facilitation shown on the next page. You may want to review your own style and see how many 'dos' you achieve and whether you show any of the 'don'ts'.

DO	DON'T
• Plan and prepare • Manage the time and the environment • Acknowledge and build on ideas • Summarise and test understanding • Encourage participation • Protect the weak • Control the strong • Keep the energy high • Manage conflict	• Allow outside interruptions • Dominate • Give your opinion first • Compete with team members (or allow them to compete with each other) • Take sides • Immediately focus on the flaws in the other's argument • Argue • Manipulate • Be dismissive, condescending or sarcastic (or allow others to be)

For more on facilitation take a look at Chapters 15–17 which focus on creating positive conversations, holding great meetings and working in virtual and cross-cultural teams.

From facilitating to coaching your team

So far we have looked at the essential skills of coaching and facilitation. These skills can be brought together using the TOPIC framework for team coaching.

Our definition of team coaching is:

Engaging in a shared process that is focused on improving performance by developing individual and team capabilities, to achieve game-changing results.

A cornerstone of team coaching is creating a shared process, which will help to develop collaboration and more creative ways of working.

The TOPIC model (see Figure 3.4) is designed to help you to bring out the best in your team by asking good, open questions to stimulate new, innovative ideas. This process will also create commitment and buy-in as the team will be involved in creating the solution.

It is a framework which will guide you through the coaching process. It starts by creating a common understanding of the agenda or **Topic** you want to focus on, and then moves on to agreeing the **Outcomes** you all want to achieve. The model then allows the team to share information by exploring the **Present** situation, before looking creatively at all the possible **Ideas** and, finally, focusing on the **Conclusion** and plans to move forward.

Figure 3.4 Essential skills of coaching

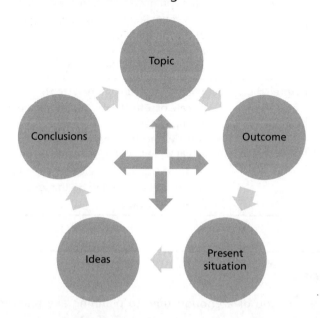

You can also use this framework as a problem-solving process in a team meeting and allocate time to each part of the model, so that the whole team can work together to coach each other.

Use the framework below to help you and the team to get started.

Topic	Clarify the topic you want to focus on	What would you like to discuss? Is there any specific aspect you would like to focus on? What is really important to you right now? Is everyone in agreement?
Outcome	Focus on the outcomes	What do we want to achieve? What will it be like when we get there? What is acceptable to us all? What time scale can we set for achieving this? How will we measure our success?
Present situation	Explore the current situation	What has been done so far? How have things gone? Where are we right now with x? Has anyone ever tackled anything like this in the past? Is there anyone who can help us? What can help us to move forward?

▶

Ideas	Generate ideas and options	So what could we do to achieve our outcome? What is your view of the best option? What do you think of x's opinion? What are you noticing? What else could we do?
Conclusion	Agree the next steps	So what will you do as a first step? On a scale of 1 to 10 how committed are we to moving ahead? How can we achieve this together? Who will be able to help/support us? What are the quick wins we could aim for? What else will we need to do to move forward? What are the next steps?

Top tips

- Make sure you give enough time to planning any team meeting and conference call. If it's a conference call take some extra time at the beginning to make sure everyone is clear about the aims of the meeting.

- During the meeting make sure you take time to notice what is going well in the group and what could be improved.

- Use your role to bring people in and manage the discussion in a positive way.

- Use the TOPIC coaching framework to coach the team and develop new ideas and approaches.

- Remember to review the meeting with the team and look at what went well and what could be improved on for next time.

Summary

Team coaching is not only a tool to develop your team, it is also a process for developing innovative and creative ideas with the team. In an era where collaboration within and across teams is essential, the contribution you and your team can make will be important to the overall business success of your organisation.

Think about some practical things from this chapter that you can do to help to coach and develop your team.

- Remember to pay attention not only to the task but to the processes and relationships in the team.

- Focus on maximising the positive behaviours, and minimising the behaviours that will hinder the progress of the team.

- Use this chapter to plan for the next team meeting you will be holding, and consciously think about your role as a coach and facilitator.

- Use the TOPIC framework with your team, and share the model with them as a way of organising your team meeting.

Actions from this chapter

ACTION	TIME FRAME	TEAM INVOLVEMENT	REFLECTIONS AND PROGRESS REVIEW
1.			
2.			
3.			

Understanding your team

We often spend more time interacting with people at work than we do with our family and friends. However, how well do you really know your team members? Do you understand what motivates them? Can you tell if they are enthusiastic or frustrated with what they are doing?

An important aspect of coaching your team is for both you and the team to become more aware of each other and how you all work together. One of the secrets of good team work and good team coaching is making the most of the diversity in the team. Diversity brings with it different perspectives and the opportunity for greater creativity. However it also has the potential to create conflict, misunderstanding and disagreement.

In this chapter we are focusing on one aspect of diversity, that of personality and preference, valuing individual difference while at the same time realising that the team needs to work together as a unit.

While it is important for the team to understand each other, it is equally important to manage the reputation of the team and for external stakeholders and customers to understand what the team stands for. We will be looking at how you can harvest the diversity in the team to develop a set of values and behaviours, to create a clear brand identity.

This chapter will not only help your team to understand each other and work more effectively, but also help your stakeholders and customers understand more about your team identity, by:

- analysing your team to identify its strengths and potential blind spots
- understanding and appreciating differences in the team
- developing effective ways of working together to create a unified team identity.

Figure 4.1 Internal and external issues

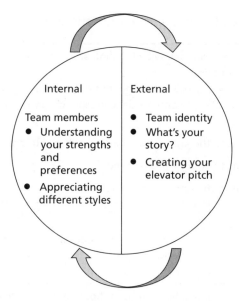

Analysing your team: the Head, Heart and Gut model

Teams consist of a variety of individuals, each with their own unique style of relating and contributing. Ashridge research into teams has created a holistic view of teams based on how individuals think, feel and act when together. This research is based on observing groups of people working in a team setting and recognising some regular patterns of behaviour that are emerging.

From our observations we have noticed that teams regularly focus on three key areas: how well they deploy their thinking power (the head preference), how much attention is paid to the relationships (the heart preference) and, finally, how much emphasis is placed on outputs, actually getting the task done (the gut preference).

The Head, Heart and Gut model allows people to discover their preferred style of working. It also helps people to be more aware of the needs of other team members. In a team coaching context this means that team members can adapt their approach and understand and appreciate the preferences of their colleagues.

Ask the team to complete the questionnaire below:

Table 4.1 The Head, Heart and Gut questionnaire

Please answer the questions below by thinking about how you typically prefer to work in a group situation.
Write your score for each word in the columns A, B and C.
For all 12 statements, allocate each of the corresponding three answers a score using the points scale below:

- Allocate 3 points to the answer that best describes your preferred style.

- Allocate 2 points to your next preference.

- Allocate 1 point to the remaining answer.

		A	B	C
1	Typically I like group situations to be	exhilarating	methodical	harmonious
2	When working in groups I like to	be adventurous	follow rules	allow for openness
3	Under pressure I am likely to be	courageous	rational	concerned
4	In a group situation I rely upon	instinct	thinking	feeling

▶

5	People would say of me when I am working in a group that I am good at	risk-taking	being objective	being passionate
6	I prefer working in groups which are	spontaneous	planned	co-operative
7	As a group member, I consider myself to be	impulsive	logical	considerate
8	I am most engaged when the focus is on	achieving the goal	intellectual aspects	the relationship aspect of group working
9	My contribution to the group is	being practical	being analytical	having empathy
10	I pride myself in being	innovative	precise	co-operative
11	I see my role in the group as one who is	driving the task forward	seeking the truth	actively encouraging
12	I like groups that are focused on being	imaginative	factual	appreciative
	Add up the scores you gave for each column:	A – Total:	B – Total:	C – Total:

Interpreting your results

It is assumed that we are able to display all of the behaviours when working in groups, but we may favour one style over another. The descriptions below may give you some insights into how you prefer to work in teams. You may find you identify with more than one style.

The column/box you scored the highest number in is likely to be your strongest preference. Please read the preference descriptions below:

Gut – Column A

People with a preference for Gut behaviour may notice they have a strong urge to be busy doing something. They may find that they adopt a 'hands-on' approach to problem-solving. They are more prone than others to make risky decisions and enjoy teams that allow them to be impulsive and spontaneous. Often in groups they may act on a 'gut feel' but may find it hard to articulate why they know an idea will work, it just will.

Potential weakness: Teams that have lots of Gut people may notice that they have lots of ideas, but may struggle to stay focused on formulating a plan, and owing to their hands-on approach may lose some of their excellent ideas.

Head – Column B

People who favour Head behaviour may recognise a preference for logical, rational analysis of the problem or task, and their input will focus upon thinking about how to solve the problem. They may be at their most comfortable when they are able to analyse the situation, and may strive to create a plan.

Potential weakness: Teams that have a high number of people who favour 'Head' may tend to ask lots of questions at the start of the tasks, striving to get clarity on fine detail. They work more easily with truth and fact than ambiguity. Head people tend to have strength when it comes to formulating excellent plans, but can sometimes find themselves running out of time when it comes to the implementing phase.

Heart – Column C

Those who identify with Heart behaviour may find they are more concerned with the feelings of the group, and may notice that they are happiest in groups that have harmony. They typically invest their energy in nurturing the relationships within the group, which may be demonstrated through encouraging, offering support and showing

▶

appreciation of the contributions of others. They may find themselves noticing when people are unhappy or are excluded from decisions or conversations, and may attempt to include them.

Potential weakness: Teams that have a high number of Heart people create warm and empathetic environments to work in, but they risk not being able to make a decision for fear of offending others in the team.

Insight

One team leader we interviewed remarked:

> I recognised myself in this questionnaire: I am definitely 'head'. With me it's just facts, facts, facts, and I forget sometimes that not everyone is the same as me. With quite a lot of people in my team who are 'heart' I recognised I needed a change of approach. No wonder our meetings are lacking energy! I made a conscious effort to understand some of the people issues involved in our decisions and showed more appreciation for people's efforts. I am struck by the difference it has made to the mood of our team meetings. It doesn't take a lot of time, but the benefits have been substantial. We still need data, but I think about how I present it and include other people's views more.

TAKE AWAY

Consider how your own style varies from others in your team.

USING THE QUESTIONNAIRE

When the team has completed the questionnaire, plot the results on a flip chart (see Figure 4.2). Take the highest score for each individual and write their name in the corresponding 'domain' of Head, Heart or Gut. If you have two high scores plot them both on the chart.

Figure 4.2 The Head, Heart and Gut chart

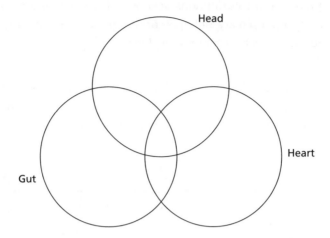

ANALYSING YOUR RESULTS: IDEAS FOR DISCUSSION

Using the data in Table 4.1 and the descriptions in Table 4.2, discuss the results.

Table 4.2 Characteristics of the Head, Heart and Gut preferences

HEART	HEAD	GUT
Building relationships	Objective focus	Focus on the goal and
Trust	Clear outcomes	outputs
Communication	Analytical	Developing a sense of
Collaboration	Processes	urgency, energy and
Consensus	Rational	drive
Feedback	Define responsibilities	Action oriented
Listening	Decision-making	Impulsive
Celebrating success	Low (or considered) risks	Challenging
		Risk-taking

- What are the strengths in the team?
- What are the blind spots?
- What are the implications for this both within the team and with other stakeholders?
- What insights does this give into the way the team interacts and makes decisions?
- Is there anything you need to change or do differently as a team?

Remember, this is not a psychometric questionnaire. Team members should be encouraged to work in all three domains, moving around them as the context requires. Having a low score in any domain is not licence to ignore using the style! In fact you will gain much more from experimenting and trying out a new approach.

DEVELOPING EFFECTIVE WAYS OF WORKING TOGETHER: CASE EXAMPLE

A team leader in a charitable organisation used this questionnaire with her team and realised that they had predominantly Heart and Head preferences (see Figure 4.3).

Figure 4.3 Team data from a charitable organisation

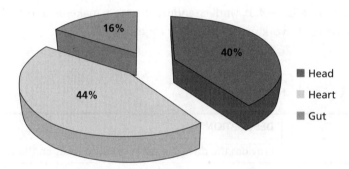

It was clear that the team worked well together. Their discussion showed that they were considerate of others, listened well and there was a high degree of trust and support. The team was also quite analytical with some team members focusing on the planning and detail. However there was very little Gut thinking in the group and this meant that often the team fell behind on timelines.

Subsequently, the team agreed to hold regular meetings and conference calls. If someone had an action to complete before the next meeting, it was expected that they would make sure the task was done in time.

As a 'Head' person, the team leader also realised that she needed to be more people focused. As first she found it strange, but soon saw the benefits:

> I find all this praising and listening to others a bit hard if I'm honest . . . at first I thought 'I haven't got time for this', but I have to say it really does get results, my team do seem to have been a lot more engaged recently . . . it is worth the extra effort.

From a team coaching perspective all three preferences are important in achieving a great outcome and teams need to develop the agility to work with each other to maximise their potential.

An alternative approach

Whilst the Head, Heart and Gut model is something you can use with your team to explore their preferred style of working, there are other questionnaires which focus on different areas important to team performance.

The Belbin questionnaire[1] looks at the roles people play in the team. Through his research with teams, Belbin identified nine roles that people can display in a team setting (see Table 4.3). Understanding the team make-up and preferences can help the team work more effectively together.

Table 4.3   Belbin team roles

TEAM ROLES	DESCRIPTION
Shaper	Provides the drive the team needs to focus on the task
Co-ordinator	Focuses on the objectives and how the task is achieved. They are usually good at delegating
Team worker	Helps the team to gel and is aware of the people issues and morale in the team
Implementer	Is good at getting the job done, and is logical and practical in approach
Resource investigator	Looks outside the team for insights and resources and prevents the team from being too inward focused
Plant	Is creative, often thinking outside the box and bringing different ideas to the team
Monitor evaluator	Is good at evaluating the decisions and ideas in the team, taking a logical and dispassionate focus
Completer finisher	Has attention to detail and will want the team to deliver high-quality solutions
Specialist	Brings specialist strength to the team

Figure 4.4 Belbin team roles grouped

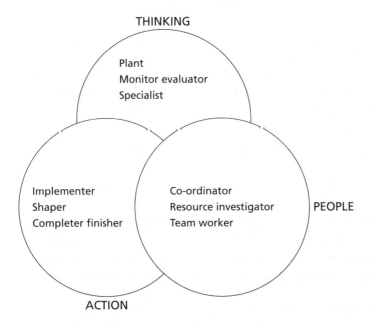

From our experience of working with and observing groups, the team roles really do play a part in how people work together as a team.

For example:

- If there are too many shapers in a team, beware. Whilst they bring energy and drive to the team, they can also lead to conflict if they are competing for power.
- A lack of completer finishers can mean that whilst the team may complete the task, they will not have paid much attention to the quality of the result
- Monitor evaluators are very helpful in questioning and thinking through ideas, but too many in a team can lead to analysis paralysis.

Each of the Belbin roles has unique strengths and the challenge is to recognise the strengths, use them well and compensate for any missing roles. Completing the profile and sharing the results in the team is a great way to discuss the team strengths, look at potential problem areas which could (or do) arise in the team, and identify how to manage them.

You can find out more about the Belbin team roles and gain access to the Belbin questionnaire at **www.Belbin.com**

Creating your team identity

So far in this chapter we have explored the importance of valuing and appreciating difference in the team, and now we will look at how you harness that diversity to create one cohesive team through the power of developing a team brand identity. Whether or not you have explored it, your stakeholders will have a perception of you based on your team brand identity.

THINKING ABOUT YOUR TEAM AS A BRAND

We often think of brands associated with products and services, but this concept is equally applicable to the team. A brand identity delivers a promise and helps you to communicate with your key stakeholders, as well as helping the team align around a set of values. Done well, it will help you gain the right kind of recognition. This section will offer you some ideas for how to create even greater team cohesion through developing a team brand so that you can create:

- a clear purpose and direction
- a cohesive message that you will communicate consistently to all your stakeholders
- a level of control about how you are viewed by other stakeholders
- an increased sense of team belonging and motivation
- a team that is better prepared to deliver game-changing results.

GETTING STARTED

When we talk about branding in this context, we are not talking about a cosmetic facelift, a new shiny logo or team mascots and T-shirts. What we are suggesting is that you and the team develop a deeper understanding of your team values, to ask the important question: 'What are we in the service of?' This will help you to align your systems, processes, team behaviour and communication channels around a clear brand identity.

A good place to start is to understand how you are currently perceived. Engage the team in meeting with key stakeholders and find out what they want. What are you currently doing that works well? What else needs to be done? Where is the focus of your energy? Once you have gathered this information, come back together and discuss as a whole team in order to define your identity and how to communicate it.

Figure 4.5 Your team brand identity

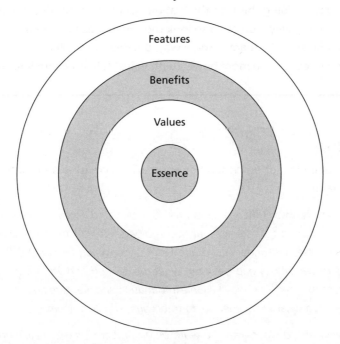

DEVELOPING A BRAND IDENTITY

If you think about any brand, it is made up of what is known as the brand essence: the core element of the brand and what it stands for. This is then expressed through the values, benefits and features of the product or service (see Figure 4.5).

Try this

Get together with your team and explore:

- **Your brand essence.** What do you stand for as a team? (Sometimes it's easier to do this by looking for images and visuals that express your team identity.)

- **Your values.** What is important to you and your customers?

- **The benefits you offer.** What are the services and deliverables you offer to others?

- **The features.** What behaviours and approach can the team use to support your brand identity and communicate it to others?

▶

A fun way of doing this is to think about what car or product your team would be and why. You can also look though magazines and find images which represent the team in some way. Building up a collage of images is sometimes easier and more powerful than just talking about your brand.

Insight

A new team leader described her approach to creating a brand identity in the team:

> When I took over the team I wanted to understand how we were perceived and what sort of service our stakeholders wanted from us. The team themselves felt undervalued and were undervalued by our stakeholders. There was also a gap between what we offered and what our external clients wanted. This was valuable information and we were able to use it to focus on what we needed to do to become a brilliant team.

> I went on to work with the team on a number of levels, including small things such as changing our language. We now talk about 'upping our game' and see ourselves as a 'team'. We have also established our vision and identity, which is: We want to provide an excellent service in all we do and work with passion, professionalism and pride.

> We have now set up three groups to work on uniting the team, enhancing our relationships with our stakeholders and improving our client offering. We've also set up an 'inspiration board' where we can post feedback, insights and photographs, and create an understanding of what being a brilliant team means.

TAKE AWAY

Get feedback from your stakeholders and use this to work with the team to create a clear brand identity.

Story telling

Another way to explore the team's core values and identity is through stories. Just like brands, stories engage emotions.

Stories can:

- emotionally connect people together
- help to foster collaboration
- create a sense of community
- inform you of the values you hold and how people work
- be memorable and passed on as anecdotes.

Try this

At your next team meeting start with getting people to share some stories about what they have been working on or what successes they have had. It's important that everyone gives their full attention. At the end you can discuss the key messages that express what you stand for as a team.

Once you have done this, you can think about how you condense your story into a short 'elevator pitch'.

DESIGNING AN ELEVATOR PITCH

An elevator pitch is a short, snappy description about the team. It is crafted specifically to be memorable and engaging for the listener.

The pitch should tell the listener what your team does, their values and uniqueness.

Insight

The manager of a conference centre talked about how he created the team brand identity and client experience at his venue:

> To start with we don't talk about 'personnel', we talk about 'the team' and our vision is to give all our clients the warmest welcome we can. Our conference centre is like a home and we all work to create this atmosphere. I talk to my team about the inverted pyramid where the customer is our

▶

boss and we always have their needs in mind. These values mean that we are always trying to do small things to please and surprise the participants and we all get involved in the process from organising themed events to helping out in any way we can. All the staff eat together, so we share stories and support each other. We also meet each week to discuss the clients, so that we understand their needs and what we can do to make their stay special.

The team's elevator pitch 'to provide the warmest welcome possible' means that they:

- make sure the participants are welcomed on arrival
- place all the photographs of the team in the hall with their names
- learn the first names of the participants
- remember birthdays and go out of their way to create small surprises
- work as a team to create the feeling of being looked after
- are involved in coming up with new and creative ideas
- take pride in what they do.

TAKE AWAY
Develop your brand identity into in actions and behaviours through the stories you tell, and create an elevator pitch which everyone can use.

Try this

You can create your elevator pitch with the team. If you have a larger team, break into smaller groups. Using sticky notes and flip charts, have the team write as many things as possible to answer the following questions:

- What do you want to communicate?
- What is the purpose or function of the team?
- What does the team do?
- What are your team values and how do you express them?
- What is special about your team?

Once you have developed the brand identity and elevator pitch, think about how you live the brand values through your team behaviour. You can break down your elevator pitch into smaller chunks and brainstorm the behaviours that are aligned to your message. Table 4.4 provides some ideas using excerpts from existing elevator pitches.

Table 4.4 Your elevator pitch

ELEVATOR PITCH	ENSUING BEHAVIOURS
'Customer first and foremost'	• Fast response to customer contact • Courteous service and personal touch • Going the extra mile to deliver customer service both internal and external • Delivering on promises • Done with a smile, genuine care
'Quality assured every time'	• Organised and structured • Detail is checked, high value attached to things looking and being high quality, including the workspace • Taking time to really understand what stakeholders need from you in order to get it right first time
'We deliver on our promises'	• Speed of service • Never late for a deadline • High energy in the team • Clearly displayed information that everyone can track • Fast-acting and efficient

Make sure you regularly check in with your stakeholders that you are delivering on your promises. Monitor the quality and feedback on what the team does. Seek feedback, both positive and developmental, and circulate this to the team so you can make sure you are living your brand values on a daily basis.

Top tips

- Spend time getting to know your team and build in time to find out more about them as individuals and as a team.
- If you work virtually, make sure you build time into your conference calls to introduce new team members and ensure that people get to

know each other. You can always use the Head, Heart and Gut model to think about better ways of working together.

- Use the Head, Heart and Gut model to think about how you behave with other teams, e.g. if you are presenting to a group of more senior managers think about their style and preference and adjust the way you present your ideas accordingly.

- Make sure you share something about yourself with the team. It's important that the team knows who you are as well.

- Spend time to create a team brand identity and develop a clear elevator pitch that is consistently delivered by everyone in the team.

Summary

In this chapter we have looked at the importance of understanding the team and the individual team members. Whether your team is a long-standing team or a temporary project team pulled together for a specific task, it is important that you understand the way you all work, the contributions each team member brings and how you can maximise the differences in the team to become more effective in the way you work, as well as harnessing that difference to create a cohesive team brand.

Think about some ideas and actions you can take forward.

Actions from this chapter

ACTION	TIME FRAME	TEAM INVOLVEMENT	REFLECTIONS AND PROGRESS REVIEW
1.			
2.			
3.			

Mapping your team

In the previous chapter we looked at the individual team members and how their different styles and preferences come together to build an effective team. This chapter considers the design and structure of your team. Teams are becoming more and more complex, often working at a distance, across time zones and cultures. In addition teams are having to learn to be more agile. They are often bought together for a specific purpose and have to develop quickly in order to deliver results.

This chapter will help you:

- to understand the type of team you are working in
- to identify the factors which will help you to become a high-performing team
- to accelerate the development and performance of your team.

Mapping your team – getting started

There are three important elements you need to consider in order to understand the overall framework in which your team operates. These are:

1. The **conditions** which help your team to flourish
2. The **context** your team is working in
3. The **capability** of the team to work and perform as a team

Figure 5.1 Mapping your team

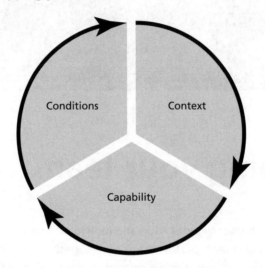

THE CONDITIONS WHICH SUPPORT TEAM PERFORMANCE

There are certain conditions which characterise a high performance team.

P – They have a clear **purpose** which everyone has bought into.

A – They rely on each other and demonstrate mutual **accountability**.

R – They have clear **roles and responsibilities**.

C – They have a **commitment** to grow and perform as a team.

S – They have different but complementary **skills**.

Figure 5.2 The PARCS model for high-performing teams

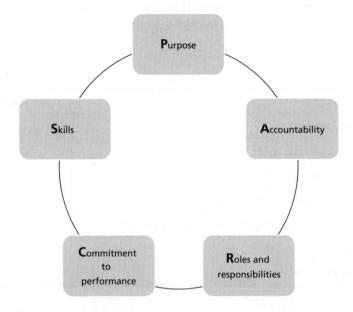

It's worth thinking about whether you are in fact working as a team or just a group of individuals. Not all groups need to work as teams. It is the element of mutual accountability which drives the need to be a team – how much you all rely on each others' skills, knowledge and support to achieve the goal.

Think about your own team and assess whether you have all the attributes of the PARCS model as they are all essential if you are going to develop into a high-performing team. Chapter 7 will help you to develop your purpose and roles and responsibilities, and the 'Focus on people' section will help you to build the potential and commitment in the team.

Understanding the context you are working in

The context and complexity of your team will influence how you work together. Look at the table on the next page and tick the team characteristics which relate to your team. Each characteristic will have an impact on the team and how you work together.

In a survey of 300 team leaders we found that 95% of our sample had three or more different team characteristics to juggle. The results also indicated a move to working in more dispersed teams which often operate across cultures and time zones[1].

TEAM CHARACTERISTICS	YOUR TEAM
Multidisciplinary	
Working across time zones	
Dispersed geographically	
Spread across organisational boundaries	
Temporary teams, put together for a specific project	
Multicultural	
Multigenerational	

Make a note of the specific characteristics of your team. Each team characteristic brings with it advantages and also potential challenges as indicated in the table below. This table is just a starter to help you think about the context in which your team operates. If you want to look more deeply into this area, refer to Chapter 17 which focuses specifically on working with virtual and cross-cultural teams.

Table 5.1 Advantages and challenges – and some ideas

Multidisciplinary		
Advantages	**Challenges**	**Ideas for you and your team**
• Brings together ideas and people from different professional backgrounds	• May be difficult to make decisions • Team members may not appreciate or understand each other's perspective	• Make sure people understand each other's role and contribution to the team • Allow time for people to share their views and ideas but be sure to summarise and draw the discussion to a conclusion ▶

Working across time zones		
Advantages	**Challenges**	**Ideas for you and your team**
• Brings a global and cross-cultural perspective to the group • May allow the team to work continually on the project	• Difficulty in getting the team together • Difficulty in communication and planning conference calls • May experience language and cultural issues	• It is really important that team members understand each other and their role in the team, so build in time for this • Plan and schedule calls that work for everyone and share the late/early morning calls • Develop systems and processes to manage information sharing

Dispersed geographically		
Advantages	**Challenges**	**Ideas for you and your team**
• Creates a broader perspective and is often closer to the customer	• Communication, understanding and building a team spirit	• Create a communication strategy which ensures regular communication • Make the most of virtual communication tools and try to reduce travel time • Make sure that the team is clear on the purpose, goals and their role in the team • Encourage the team to communicate and support each other

Spread across organisational boundaries		
Advantages	**Challenges**	**Ideas for you and your team**
• Brings a real organisational and client perspective to the team	• May be difficult to organise and there may potentially be political issues to deal with • There may be different agendas and ways of working	• Be clear about the meetings and progress reviews • Be open about the challenges and potential problems the team may face • Review each meeting and be clear about any areas of misunderstanding or disagreement • Be aware of the wider organisation and identify any stakeholders you may need to involve

▶

Temporary teams bought together for a specific project		
Advantages	**Challenges**	**Ideas for you and your team**
• These teams often have a clear focus and purpose	• Team members may not know each other • They may have a short time frame to deliver the project • They may be working on other projects at the same time	• Build in time for team members to get to know each other and agree how you will work together • Manage the expectations of external stakeholders and support the team to deliver • Be clear about individual roles, responsibilities and time commitments • Build in clear review points to monitor progress and review how the team is working together

Multicultural		
Advantages	**Challenges**	**Ideas for you and your team**
• This brings with it the potential for greater creativity and new perspectives	• Language problems • Misunderstandings about working preferences and behaviours can hinder team development	• Be aware of any language difficulties and make sure people talk clearly on conference calls and in meetings • Share some of the cultural expectations and differences and make sure everyone is involved

Multigenerational		
Advantages	**Challenges**	**Ideas for you and your team**
• Different experiences, perceptions, understanding and skills	• Frustration can arise through different expectations, ways of working and technical know-how	• It is important that the team learns to appreciate and value each other's skills • Setting up a mentoring programme and allocating tasks and roles to match the skills can help • It's also important to be clear about the expectations and ways of working and communicating in the team

In addition to thinking about the characteristics of your team, it is also important to think about its size and the overall reporting structure:

- The ideal size for a team is between eight and ten people. Any bigger and the team can become unwieldy and difficult to manage unless you set up sub-teams with team leaders.
- If your team members don't report directly to you and can only allocate a percentage of their time, you will need to work hard to create a team identity and gain commitment from the individual members. They will need to buy in to the purpose and outcome of the team and their role in it.

Insight

One team leader, faced with the new challenge of leading an international team, realised that he had to adapt his leadership approach:

With a five-hour time zone difference, there are only a few hours in the afternoon where the whole team is present. We schedule weekly calls and make good use of video conferencing tools. We have also set up shared folders so we can work on and share material. I organised a team introduction session where everyone shared a PowerPoint slide about themselves and their culture. I think it is important that we get to know each other. I also try to make sure we have clear agendas and minutes as it's important everyone understands what has been agreed.

TAKE AWAY

Make sure you take into account the type of team you are working with and adapt the ways you work together to the needs of the team.

The development stage of your team

As well as thinking about the structural make-up of the team, it is important to consider their experience and the length of time they have been together. Often, newly formed teams overlook the importance of understanding how to work together.

HOW RECENTLY HAS YOUR TEAM FORMED?

A popular way of looking at the stages teams go through was developed by Bruce Tuckman[2] who identified four stages in team development (see Figure 5.3). The *forming stage* is where there is usually a high level of morale as the team members get to know each other. They then often go through what is known as a *storming* phase where people are establishing their roles and their views about what to do. This is often a difficult but important stage for the team. It can lead into developing some norms and processes about how the team should work together and move forward. This is known as the *norming stage* and, following this, teams usually move into a stage where they *perform* well and have built the trust and understanding to work together. The final stage, known as *adjourning,* is often applicable to projects where the task is complete and the team disbands and moves on.

Figure 5.3 The Tuckman team stages model

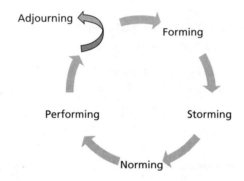

As a team coach it is important to recognise the stage your team is in and provide facilitation and support to help them move through the different stages. It's also important to remember that any change in the team, such as a new team member, shifting goalposts and organisational changes, can influence the developmental stage of the team.

Use Table 5.2 to identify the development stage of your team, and the ideas and actions you could take to help the team work towards the performance phase.

Described on the following pages are two examples which illustrate how important it is to understand and help your team to work through the various development stages. The first describes a newly formed team, and the second a team which is established but disillusioned and not functioning well.

Table 5.2 Identifying the development stage of your team

STAGE	SIGNS
Forming	Roles and relationships are established. People are being polite and starting to get to know each other. **Action:** Provide opportunities for the team to get to know each other better through team development days and social gatherings and make sure everyone has plenty of information about the purpose and goal of the team.
Storming	There is potential for some conflict as people begin to establish their position in the team and understanding of their role. **Action:** Do not avoid this stage. Your role is to coach and facilitate the team to work through some of the challenges and issues they are facing. Try to use some of the techniques from Chapters 3 and 4 to help the team to understand each other and discuss the issues in a positive way.
Norming	The team are ready to create some norms and ways of working together. **Action:** Create a team charter (described in the next section (see pages 86–7) to establish ways of working and ground rules. Review these regularly with your team. Your aim is to help the team learn to manage themselves so that you can support them.
Performing	The team are operating well, there is a high level of trust and support and they are progressing well with the task. **Action:** Step back and leave the team space to get on with the job. Do not micromanage. Instead, use your time to pave the way for the team, through engaging stakeholders, overcoming barriers and developing strategic direction.
Adjourning	A team member leaves or the team is split. A period of grieving may be experienced. **Action:** Allow people to mark significant occasions. Celebrate success and encourage the team to provide feedback to each other. Capture what went well and what could be improved so that you can all take the learning on to the next team or project.

Insight 1

Sacha is a project manager with a team of six people pulled together from different parts of the organisation to complete a project. She had 'one-to-one' coaching conversations with each team member to discuss their development needs and understand more about their skills and abilities. She also used the Head, Heart and Gut model with the team and facilitated a session where they could share their strengths, and understand each other's preferences and ways of working. As this was a new team she wanted to build trust and understanding as quickly as possible.

Sacha also realised that, for the project to be a success, the team needed to work effectively together to leverage its joint skills and resources. She used the TOPIC model with the team to agree outcomes for the project, to share and understand more about the context they were working in, and to work creatively together to reflect on how they could achieve the outcome within the time scales.

TAKE AWAY

Take time to help the team to form and create a clear understanding of what they need to achieve. Help to coach and facilitate them through this process.

Insight 2

Raj joined an existing team as a new team leader. He quickly realised that the team was not working effectively. They were demoralised and feeling bruised following a reorganisation in the department.

This presented a real challenge. Initially Raj led from the front. He provided the team members with clear roles and responsibilities and deliverables, and gave them the autonomy to run their area. He provided lots of support and practical help, and was very hands-on. Weekly meetings were used to share ideas and concerns and gradually all the team members became more vocal and involved.

A real breakthrough for Raj was when one of the team had a problem and emailed his colleagues, who all responded immediately even though

▶

it was out of office hours. 'I realised that the team were committed and had started to work together, which is what we needed to succeed. I could now step back and support them.'

TAKE AWAY

Analyse the situation. At the early stages of team development you may need to be more hands-on and coach the team to develop their confidence.

Mapping your team

A useful way of pulling the ideas together about your team is to map your team, using the chart below. This will provide a starting point to think about how you can best support them.

MAPPING THE TEAM	IDEAS AND ACTIONS
Conditions Refer back to the PARCS model (Figure 5.2). In which areas does your team do well? What do you need to work on?	
Context Think about the context and characteristics of your team (Table 5.1). How does this impact on team performance? What can you do to support the team?	
Capabilities What development level is your team operating at (Figure 5.3)? What can you do to help them to grow into a high-performing team?	

Top tips

- Analyse the characteristics of your team. Different teams need different approaches depending on their formation.
- Discuss the potential challenges with the team and create solutions together.

▶

- Regularly review the progress with your team. Consider what is working well and how can you improve.
- Recognise the development stage of your team and help them move towards becoming a high-performing team.
- Don't use a one-size-fits-all approach to working with teams. They are complex and fluid structures which can easily fall apart if you don't adapt and flex your approach as team leader.

Summary

It is so easy for teams to fail if they are too unwieldy and don't have a structure and design that enables them to work together effectively. We have seen in Chapter 4 and in this chapter that as a team coach you need to recognise the skills and preferences of your team and work together to build a structure which enables everyone to communicate more effectively and achieve their potential. Part two will provide you with plenty of tools and techniques to help you work on any of the challenges you may have identified.

Actions from this chapter

ACTION	TIME FRAME	TEAM INVOLVEMENT	REFLECTIONS AND PROGRESS REVIEW
1.			
2.			
3.			

Getting started

This chapter will look at the practicalities of how to get started with coaching your team. We have now covered many of the skills associated with coaching your team and also provided some questionnaires, suggestions, top tips and ideas to reflect on the different aspects of team working and coaching.

Here we will provide you with the opportunity to look back and assess your progress in developing your key skills. We will also help you to assess your team's performance and identify the areas you may want to work on over the coming months.

This chapter will support you in:

- reviewing your progress as a team coach
- reviewing the performance of your team
- getting the team on board
- getting started – creating your team coaching agenda.

Reviewing your progress

Looking back over the first part of this book, we have covered a broad range of skills associated with leading, coaching and understanding teams, all of which create 'The team coach's toolkit'.

Figure 6.1 Team coach's toolkit

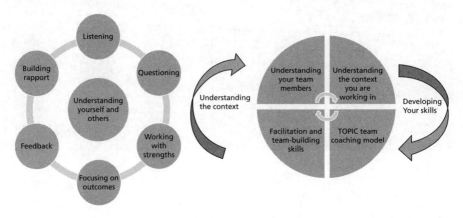

Figure 6.2 Overview of Part one

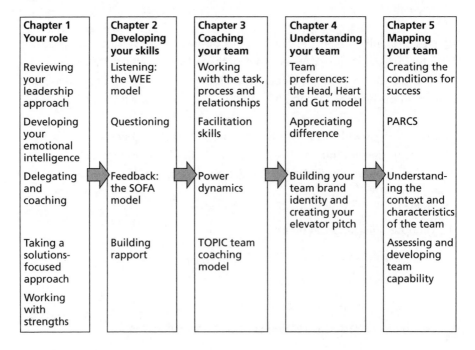

Chapter 1 Your role	Chapter 2 Developing your skills	Chapter 3 Coaching your team	Chapter 4 Understanding your team	Chapter 5 Mapping your team
Reviewing your leadership approach	Listening: the WEE model	Working with the task, process and relationships	Team preferences: the Head, Heart and Gut model	Creating the conditions for success
Developing your emotional intelligence	Questioning	Facilitation skills	Appreciating difference	PARCS
Delegating and coaching	Feedback: the SOFA model	Power dynamics	Building your team brand identity and creating your elevator pitch	Understanding the context and characteristics of the team
Taking a solutions-focused approach	Building rapport	TOPIC team coaching model		Assessing and developing team capability
Working with strengths				

REVIEW OF PART ONE

Use the personal skills assessment tool below (Table 6.1 and the questions that follow) to reflect on what you have taken away and applied from this part of the book.

Use a scale of 1–5 where:

1 = Never

2 = Rarely

3 = Sometimes

4 = Often

5 = Always

Circle your answer.

Table 6.1 Looking back over Part one

	YOUR ASSESSMENT 1 2 3 4 5
I encourage the team to develop ideas rather than always trying to come up with the answer myself.	1 2 3 4 5
I take a solution-focused approach and work with the strengths of others.	1 2 3 4 5
I listen to what others have to say and build rapport.	1 2 3 4 5
I make a point of giving regular, balanced feedback to team members.	1 2 3 4 5
I plan well for team meetings and think about how to facilitate and involve team members.	1 2 3 4 5
I use the TOPIC coaching models with the team.	1 2 3 4 5
I have a good understanding of the preferences and styles of team members (head/heart/gut).	1 2 3 4 5
I am aware of my own preferences and how this affects the team.	1 2 3 4 5
I am aware of what type of team I am working with.	1 2 3 4 5
I am aware of the development level of my team.	1 2 3 4 5

What have been the most important messages, skills or ideas that you have taken away?

How have you been able to apply this learning with your team and what results have you seen?

LEARNING	HOW HAVE YOU APPLIED THIS?	WHAT WAS THE RESULT?

Are there any aspects of Part one that you need to refer back to for your own development?

You may want to refer back to the relevant chapters, and work though some of the activities and questionnaires. It may also be useful for you to look at the recommended resources at the end of the book for more ideas.

The U-SHAPER model can act as a checklist and reminder you of what you need to be a good team coach:

U-SHAPER model for team performance

U   **Understand** the outcome

S   Provide **support**

H   Demonstrate **honesty** with yourself and honesty to those you are coaching

A   Be **action** and outcome focused, so that everyone is clear about what will happen next

P   **Prepare** well for everything you do with the team

E   Demonstrate **enthusiasm** and **energy**

R   **Review** progress on a regular basis

Reviewing the performance of your team

You may have some ideas about the team strengths and development areas of your team gained from Chapter 5, but it is really useful to develop this analysis with your team so that everyone has a clear perception about how you need to develop in the future.

Part two is based on a model for team success which focuses on three key elements of successful team performance: outcomes, people and communication (see Figure 6.3).

Figure 6.3 The three focus elements

The questionnaire (see Table 6.2) will help you to review the performance of the team and identify where you need to focus your coaching efforts.

USING THE TEAM PERFORMANCE QUESTIONNAIRE

1 Ask each of the team members to complete the questionnaire individually.
2 Chart up the scores against each question on a flip chart.
3 Discuss the results.

   - Which questions do you all score highly on? What does this tell you about the team strengths?
   - Which questions produced low scores? What can you do to enhance performance in these areas?

Table 6.2 Team performance questionnaire

		PLEASE SCORE EACH STATEMENT ON A FIVE-POINT SCALE: 1 MEANS STRONGLY DISAGREE AND 5 MEANS STRONGLY AGREE	
1	The team has a clear sense of purpose.	
2	Team members are in agreement about the outputs, deliverables and time scales.	
3	Team members are clear about their roles and contribution to the team.	
4	The team works well with other areas in the organisation.	
5	The team respond well and adapt to changes which impact on their performance.	
6	All team members are motivated and engaged.	
7	The team support each other, especially when working under pressure.	
8	Performance issues in the team are handled well.	
9	The team regularly reviews its performance.	
10	The individual performance of team members is reviewed on a regular basis.	
11	Team members communicate on a regular basis with each other.	
12	Team meetings are always productive and worthwhile.	
13	When conflict arises it is managed well.	
14	Team members have the opportunity to share ideas and feel listened to.	
15	The team communicates well with external stakeholders.	

FOCUS ON OUTCOMES

Questions 1–5 are concerned with the **outcomes** from the team and refer to having a clear purpose, vision and direction. This needs to be shared by the team so that everyone is moving in the same direction. However, the outputs of the team must also fit in with the overall strategy and be communicated to the wider organisation. Collaborating with others, managing performance and working in a constantly changing environment are all aspects that influence the effectiveness of the team in delivering results. Chapters 7–10 will provide ideas, suggestions and top tips to develop this area of your team. See Figure 6.4.

Figure 6.4 Focus on outcomes

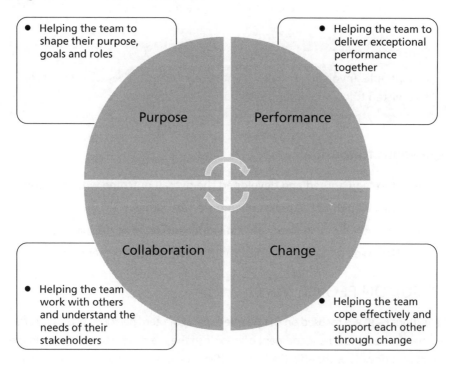

- Helping the team to shape their purpose, goals and roles

- Helping the team to deliver exceptional performance together

Purpose

Performance

Collaboration

Change

- Helping the team work with others and understand the needs of their stakeholders

- Helping the team cope effectively and support each other through change

Insight

A general manager we worked with described his approach to building a common, shared outcome during the strategic review process:

> We had two meetings to focus on the strategic review. I started by setting direction and inspiring them to take a broader perspective. I wanted to take people away from their day-to-day jobs. We all went off to gather data and then met again so that we could make an informed decision. We also invited the production manager to this meeting to gain his views. We had some challenging conversations; it's not always easy to get consensus. We listened to all the ideas and listed the options. Once we had reached an agreement that everyone could buy into, it was much easier for them to communicate this to the rest of the organisation because they were part of it.

TAKE AWAY

Get people involved in developing the outputs. They will be more committed to buying in to it and sharing it with others.

Questions to consider

- Have you agreed and developed the overall outcome with the team?
- How well does the team collaborate with others?
- Do you take time to review individual and team performance?
- How well does the team work with and respond to change?

FOCUS ON PEOPLE

Questions 6–10 are focused on the **people** aspects of team performance. This refers to the motivation and engagement of people in the team, how to build trust in the team and how to work effectively and efficiently in times of stress and pressure. As a team coach you have an important role in developing the performance of the individual team members so that they develop their potential and ensure that the team has the capability to meet future challenges. These topics are covered in Chapters 11–14.

Figure 6.5 Focus on people

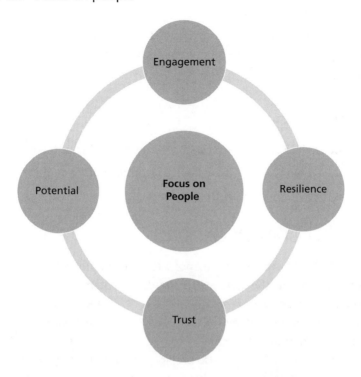

Insight

One marketing manager describes her leadership approach:

It doesn't come from anything formal. I spent the early stages of my career working in the hotel industry which is very people orientated. It was working in that environment that helped me to understand that you get the best from others if you treat them with respect. I spend about 40% of my time with the team – more at certain times of the year, such as appraisals. In my team there are a mix of people, some who are creative and others who have strong organisational skills. This can cause tensions and it's important we understand each other. We also have to work cross-functionally with people on the shop floor and in the purchasing team. It's really important to understand their constraints and work towards a common goal.

▶

Questions to consider

- How well do you know what motivates each of your team members?
- Does everyone in the team have a clear development plan?
- Are there high levels of trust in the team?

FOCUS ON COMMUNICATION

Questions 11–15 of the team performance questionnaire (Table 6.2) are concerned with **communication,** the glue which holds the team together. The more complex and dispersed your team, the more you will need to focus on creating a clear communication strategy for them (see Figure 6.6). Chapters 15–18 cover these issues, looking at how to have positive conversations and manage team conflict. This section of Part two also provides ideas for hosting great meetings, communicating effectively at a distance and across cultures and creating a communication plan which is tailored to your particular team environment.

Insight

One manager described how important team communication was for building engagement and making better decisions:

> We have a real focus on communication in our organisation. We work in an agile environment which means that I don't have a desk. I try to be available as much as I can for people. We have weekly management team briefings, one-to-one meetings and also a 'rewards and applauds' system where we recognise good ideas. One thing we are also trying is a 'Let's talk' session. This is held once a month for people of all grades to come along and share their thoughts and ideas.

TAKE AWAY

Communication not only connects the team but is essential in making decisions, developing and sharing new ideas.

Figure 6.6 Focus on communications

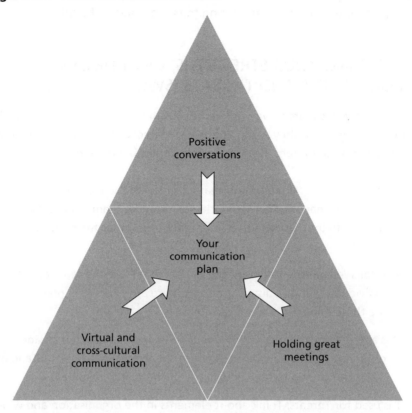

- How much time do you spend communicating with your team?
- How effective are team meetings?
- Do you have a clear and agreed communications plan?
- Have you adapted the way you communicate to the structure, preferences and needs of the team?

Getting the team on board

Building team performance and creating a team coaching environment is a multi-layered process. Whilst Part one of this book has helped you to develop your skills and expertise as a team coach, it is also important to develop the skills, expertise and commitment of the team so that they can coach and support each other. The team also needs to understand the bigger picture and recognise the opportunities and challenges facing them now and in the future.

IDENTIFYING YOUR STRENGTHS, WEAKNESSES, OPPORTUNITIES AND THREATS (SWOT)

A SWOT analysis is a great way to help the team understand more about the environment in which they work. This is a well-known framework often used for analysing organisations, but it is equally applicable to teams.

S is for Strengths. What are the characteristics of the team, or team members, that are clear strengths? What is the team good at? What do you do that distinguishes your team from other teams in the business?

W is for Weaknesses. What are the factors that place the team or individuals in it at a disadvantage? Where are your weak points, and are these minor or major disadvantages?

O is about Opportunities. Think about the opportunities in the wider organisation and environment which the team can take advantage of. What can you do to take advantage of these opportunities?

T is used for Threats. Think about elements in the organisation and wider environment, or maybe within the team, that could potentially affect your success. How can you respond to these threats?

Figure 6.7 The SWOT framework

Strengths	Weaknesses
Opportunities	Threats

Set aside some time with your team to brainstorm, discuss and agree the elements of your team SWOT. The actual process of working together on this is a useful way to engage and involve the whole team in thinking about the challenges you face (see Figure 6.7).

CHECK OUT THE TEMPERATURE IN THE TEAM

Understanding the climate of the team is important. Is it a cold, chilly environment or a warm, friendly one? The easiest way to do this is to carry out a 'team climate survey'. This is useful in a kick-off event, but can also be done periodically to ensure people are engaged and motivated. There is no limit to the questions you could pose, but probably the simplest questions you could ask are:

- What are the most rewarding aspects of being in this team?
- What are the most frustrating aspects of being in this team?
- On a scale of 1–10 (1 being not at all, and 10 being high) how motivated do you feel in this team right now?

If you haven't tried this before, it can be helpful to do this on an individual basis, and review the overall results as a team, but perhaps over time, you can work on this as part of a team meeting when you can identify how to progress on your journey to become a high-performing team.

Developing ways of working together

Now you have some information about how your team likes to work, and the opportunities and challenges you face, it is useful to develop some ground rules for the team. These should be co-created by all the team, to build a sense of personal ownership. These ground rules are often referred to as a 'team charter' and act as reference point for how the team will work. This is especially important for teams that are brought together for a specific project and for virtual teams who may not understand how their colleagues like to work. Feel free to adapt the team charter example below to your own team situation.

Insight

When I took over a new team as manager I met with each team member and asked them four questions.

- What do you enjoy?
- What do you need from me?
- What do you want to achieve?
- What would you change if you could?

These questions gave me a real insight into the climate and energy in the team and I was able to collate the responses to come up with a plan for the team moving forward.

TAKE AWAY

It's important to understand the climate in your team so you and the team can decide how to develop it.

TEAM CHARTER	
What is the purpose of this team, why are we together?	
What are the roles of each team member?	
What do good team behaviours look like?	
How will we manage conflict?	
How do we want to communicate with each other?	
What is success for the team and how will we measure it?	
How will we develop and support one another?	
What behaviours will we NOT tolerate?	

SOMETHING TO BE AWARE OF . . .

Whilst building a close-knit team is a great advantage, do be aware that you face the risk of getting caught up in 'groupthink'. This concept was created by Irving Janis. Working with groups, he noticed that the ones which made faulty decisions had some common characteristics. They were often made up of people from a similar background and were insulated from outside opinions. They failed to look at different options, or question their approach, allowing the desire for consensus to determine the decision.

A famous example of the groupthink concept was the Challenger space shuttle disaster, where the engineers knew that some parts were faulty, but the pressure to avoid negative press and keep the space race on track meant that the team went ahead even though it was the wrong decision. A more current, and most unfortunate, example is the groupthink at VW cars which resulted in some senior engineers installing switches to show false, reduced emission readings.

There are plenty of ways to avoid 'groupthink':

- Ask your customers or other teams you interact with to give you some candid feedback on the team. What do they admire about the team? And what could the team do to improve?
- Bring someone from a different part of the business into the team meeting and ask them to give their ideas and views about what the team is doing.
- Encourage team members to speak up if they have an alternative view. Make sure that their views are heard and taken seriously.
- Make sure that, as a team leader, you are open to other views and ideas.

Getting started: creating your team coaching agenda

In Chapter 6 you have had the opportunity to:

- review your own progress as a team coach

- review the performance of the team

- develop some ideas to get the team on board

- get started with your team so that you can work more effectively together.

You are now ready to start your coaching journey. Part two will provide you with a whole range of tools, techniques and ideas to help you work with your team to develop their performance.

As a first step, list the topics and challenges you have identified from the team SWOT exercise and the team performance questionnaire. This will then act as the basis for your team coaching agenda.

1

2

3

4

Also think about where the energy of the team is. What were the strengths and development areas that came out of the team climate review?

Primary focus should be on the areas which will be real game-changers for your team and will make a difference to how you work together. There are three key components of effective team work which are crucial for team success:

1 **A shared sense of purpose.** The sense of purpose is what binds the team together. It provides a focus to organise, delegate roles and responsibilities and a clear understanding for everyone to buy into.

2   **Positive working relationships.** Without this you won't have the opportunity to build the trust, support and team resilience needed to deliver game-changing results.

3   **A clear communication strategy.** Deciding how, when and what teams communicate is crucial to the success of any team, and especially so for teams who are more dispersed or working virtually.

Use these three components to prioritise your team coaching agenda and guide you as you move into the next part of this book.

Your team coaching agenda

OUTCOMES	ACTIONS	RESOURCES (WHAT RESOURCES DO YOU NEED?)	RESPONSIBILITY (WHO IS RESPONSIBLE?)	REVIEW DATES	FIRST STEPS
1.					
2.					
3.					

part two

Achieving game-changing results

Part one has provided you with some essential skills for coaching your team. Part two is designed to help you to apply these skills to a whole range of team challenges, which if tackled could achieve game-changing results.

The three focus elements

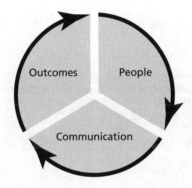

This part is split into three sections:

1 focus on outcomes
2 focus on people
3 focus on communication

Focus on outcomes

This section will provide you with the opportunity to reflect on how effective you and your team are at delivering outcomes, building performance, creating collaboration and working with change. It will provide you with plenty of suggestions, top tips, tools and ideas for you to use to coach and work with the team to deliver success.

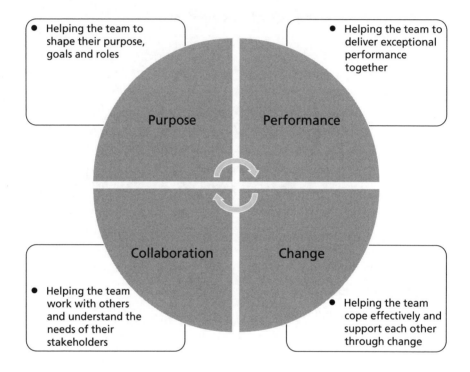

Helping the team to shape their purpose, goals and roles

Helping the team to deliver exceptional performance together

Purpose

Performance

Collaboration

Change

Helping the team work with others and understand the needs of their stakeholders

Helping the team cope effectively and support each other through change

All teams have to deliver outcomes for the wider organisation. To be effective they need to develop a clear purpose, and from there develop a set of goals and outcomes. Once you have clarity at this level it is easier to organise the team, establish well-defined roles and accountabilities, and build overall performance in the team.

Yet the life of a team is much more complex than this. All teams operate in the wider system and their success relies on the collaboration and interaction with other teams both inside and outside the organisation. Managing boundaries, building networks and relationships, and anticipating the needs of others are essential if you want to achieve a positive outcome.

To add to this complexity, teams are also operating in ever-shifting sands. Change is a constant in all our lives, and the ability to work flexibly and responsively with changing parameters and goalposts adds another dimension to everyday team work. As a team leader you need to be aware of this and work with your team to build engagement through potentially challenging situations.

Purpose, goals and roles

If your team isn't clear about its purpose, you won't be going anywhere fast. This chapter is designed to take you through the process of working with your team to develop a clear team purpose, and cascade this into clear goals, outcomes and then into team roles and accountabilities.

This chapter will allow you:

- to set a clear purpose for your team
- to establish goals and outcomes
- to develop clear roles and accountabilities.

Figure 7.1 Purpose, goals and roles for teams

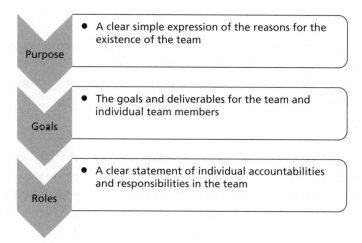

Complete the questionnaire below to assess how clear you think the team is about their purpose, goals and roles. It is also important to ask team members to complete this questionnaire individually to gain an overall perception of the team. As a team leader you may be clear about these areas, but have you shared and communicated this effectively with the team?

PLEASE SCORE ON A FIVE-POINT SCALE: 1 MEANS STRONGLY DISAGREE AND 5 MEANS STRONGLY AGREE		
	YOUR SCORE	**COMMENTS**
The team has a clear purpose.		
Everyone is aware of the goals of the team.		
Team members are clear about their own roles and responsibilities.		
Team members are aware of each other's roles and responsibilities.		
The team regularly reviews how they are performing against these goals.		
You are clear about how success will be measured in the team.		
Total		

If the average score of all the questions is:

25 or above

Your team members have a very clear understanding of the overall purpose and goals of the team and also understand their role in delivering team success. Everyone is focused in the right direction and will be regularly reviewing their performance and progress.

10–24

Your team members have some understanding of where they are heading and what they need to achieve but may not be clear on how they are going to get there. Look at the areas where you and the team achieved lower scores, and use some of the ideas in this chapter to coach the team to achieve greater clarity and understanding.

0–9

Your team really needs to focus on building a clear purpose and understand what you need to achieve and how you can work together to achieve it. You may also need to gain clarification from your manager so that you can understand how your team fits into the overall strategy and structure of the organisation.

Setting the team purpose

The starting place for any team is to develop a clear purpose. This is the guiding light that will direct the team and ensure that you all stay on track. The purpose is a commonly shared commitment and will shape what everyone does. It will ensure that team members are not just being busy, but they are being effective and channelling their energy in the right direction. Having a clear purpose also makes it easier to prioritise activities and say 'no' to requests which don't align with where you are going.

Here are some questions to think about when developing your team purpose:

- What is the team here for?
- How does this reflect the overall organisational objectives?
- What is unique about our team?
- How does what we do link into other teams?

- Who are our customers?
- How do we excel?
- What do we want to achieve?

To be successful, the team must own the purpose and the best way to do this is to develop it together. The qualities of a team purpose statement are that it:

- is short and concise – just a paragraph is enough
- is focused on the purpose of the team – the what, how and who of your team
- is memorable and clear
- encapsulates the core values, customer needs, and uniqueness of what you do
- is engaging and inspiring
- provides an overriding direction and identity for the team
- is something which is solid and is more present focused.

Insight

The head of an advertising agency described how and why they created their team purpose:

When I took over the role, the team lacked direction and were quite deflated. We also had tough targets to meet. We wanted to identify what makes us different both internally and externally and realised it was all about 'relationships': the way we work with our clients, and the way we work together. It's something we're all passionate about. We looked more at what it is about the relationships and realised we want to be innovative and stretch people's thinking. One of our clients recently gave us the feedback that 'you helped us to dream' and we need to do this all the time.

The purpose statement we came up with was to create great relationships with our clients and within the agency so that we can deliver award-winning advertising and grow the agency for the future.

This links into all our objectives and each of the team has been asked how they as a team can work to achieve this purpose.

Once agreed, make sure you keep your purpose visible. Post it up in the office or make sure that if your team is dispersed they have it somewhere where they can keep it as a visual reminder. You can also share this with your customers and other stakeholders in the organisation so that they understand more about what you all do.

Insight

One manager described his experience working on the team purpose and goals:

> We were entering into a major three-year project. To start with we developed a clear purpose and set some goals, targets and responsibilities. Eighteen months into the project we had a mid-term review to agree the plan for the next six months. Two new team members had joined the group and I was taken aback when one of them asked, 'Do we have a current vision of who we are and what we going to deliver?' We did, but it was filed away in the system.

> As a result we set up a time to review our purpose as a team and make sure that everyone on the team understood how we all fitted together. We documented it and made sure it was on the team noticeboard for all to see.

> Because the team purpose was at the forefront of my mind, I had made the mistake of thinking everyone else understood.

TAKE AWAY

Make sure your team purpose is visible and shared by all. Review it on a regular basis and make sure that new team members have a clear understanding of the team's purpose and goals.

From purpose to goals, and outcomes

Once you have worked through and agreed your team purpose, the next stage is to think about how you are going to get there. A set of clearly defined goals will help your team to focus their activities. Research has shown that 80% of conflicts in teams are attributed to unclear goals, so goal-setting needs to be an important part of the overall team coaching process.

If your goals are clear and measurable you and the team will:

- know what each person has to achieve and how this fits into the overall goal
- be able to evaluate progress
- be able to set milestones and celebrate early wins
- be able to manage conflict better as there is a common focus for any discussions
- be better able to support each other
- be motivated to achieve.

The goals should flow naturally from the purpose and vision:

- Try to focus on the top three to five goals which will make the most impact for the team. If you have too many goals you will be unlikely to achieve on all of them and will end up diluting the overall effort.
- Keep the goals simple and understandable by all: for example, a goal may be 'to build the international market by 30% in year x.' Aim to set a goal that is challenging (stretching) but one that is not impossible to achieve.
- Keep checking back to make sure the goals are aligned with your team purpose and vision.

Once you have established the goals, start to plan how you and the team can work together to achieve success:

- What are the critical success factors – the elements such as resources, time, training and support which will be critical to you moving ahead on this?

- Who are the key stakeholders you need to involve both inside and outside the team?
- What are the key measurable outcomes you want to achieve and by when?

Use the chart below to get started on this process.

Team purpose	
Team goals	
Critical success factors	
Key stakeholders	
Measurable outcomes with time frames	

KEEPING A FOCUS ON THE FUTURE

The reality of working in a team is that it can be messy; often teams have to work on multiple activities at the same time. They have to focus on the day-to-day activities as well as developing new initiatives for the future.

Baghai, Coley and White, in their book *The Alchemy of Growth*, talk about the need to focus on three horizons[1]:

Figure 7.2 Managing for the future

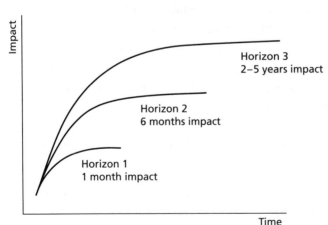

Source: Baghai, M., Coley, S., and White, D., 2000, The *Alchemy of Growth*, McKinsey & Company

1 what you need to do to have impact now

2 what you need achieve in the next six months

3 what you need to do to have impact in the next 2–5 years.

Use this framework with the team to plan out the activities you need to focus on to achieve your goals. It will help the team to manage their time and focus on the elements of their work that will deliver the most value. You also have a framework now that you can use to review your progress.

IMPACT NOW	IMPACT IN 6 MONTHS	IMPACT 2–5 YEARS

Insight

Ellen was the head of a finance team with 24 staff servicing an organisation with 1,500 employees. She recognised that the team were spending too much time on transactional work at the expense of supporting the business. The team were also feeling under stress with the amount of work they were processing.

An awayday was held which focused on looking at the core purpose for the finance team. They all agreed that their purpose was to 'to support the business by building stronger relationships and adding value through the provision of advice, support and excellent service'.

This provided a focus to explore how they were currently working and what they needed to change. They looked at the structure of the team, the task allocation, behaviours and ways of working. As a result the team reorganised around three main areas: Compliance, Business support and Adding value. This meant allocating new roles and tasks and also identifying what activities they no longer needed to do.

TAKE AWAY

Define the purpose with the team and use this to shape the goal and roles in the team.

From goals to roles

Once you have identified the purpose and goals it is much easier to identify what each team member needs to do. It is always a good idea to work with the energy of the team, so you may want to look for volunteers to take certain goals or activities forward. You may also want to focus on building collaboration across the team to enable team members to work with each other. This can work really well with dispersed teams as it is a great way of getting to know others and to learn from each other. Finally, you may want to look at the skills and development areas in the team and see the goals as development and coaching opportunities for team members.

However you and the team decide to move ahead, the important thing is that everyone knows who is doing what and by when. You will also need to think about who needs to be involved outside the team. The RACI model is a useful tool to use to make sure you have covered all aspects of achieving the goal and to ensure clarity across the team.

RACI refers to:

R – The people who are **responsible** for doing the task.

A – The person who is ultimately **accountable** and able to make decisions.

C – The people you need to **consult,** either for their expertise or approval.

I – The people you need to **keep informed** concerning progress and any implications for their area or role. This is often an area that is overlooked by teams.

Figure 7.3 illustrates how the RACI chart can be used in the team. List all the activities needed to achieve the goal down one side of the chart, and across the top identify all the people involved both inside and outside the team, and then identify their involvement by allocating a letter R-A-C-I to the relevant people. It's important to make sure that for each activity there is someone who is responsible and accountable for it.

Figure 7.3 Roles and responsibilities

Activity \ Roles											

Reviewing your progress

Once you have got started it is important to regularly review the progress of the team. Team work isn't easy and often the environment we work in is unpredictable and changing, so as a team coach the review process is central to ensuring that everyone stays on track. This process needs to be agreed with the team. As well as facilitating and coaching the team through these meetings, you may also want to schedule in some one-to-one meetings with team members so that you can provide individual coaching and support.

Insight

One country manager who works in a large multinational organisation talked about how important transparency is with regard to team goals with her senior management team. She doesn't just mean clarity between the team leader and individual team members but across the whole group:

> I have frequent discussions about goal-setting. Everyone in the team knows what our overall team goal is, as well as their individual goals. We share these so we are all aware of each other's goals. I find it's a great way to get clarity about the focus of our work and it also ensures that we are all heading in the same direction.

TAKE AWAY

Ensure that everyone is aware of the overall goal for the team and of each other's goals, to ensure you are all heading in the same direction.

Top tips

- Make sure your team has a clear, shared purpose.
- Keep the team purpose visible and refer back to it.
- Use the purpose to define the goals for the team.
- Plan activities so that the team can manage the day-to-day work and focus on the future.
- Ensure that everyone has clear roles so that they understand how they are contributing to the overall success.
- Make sure you review progress with the team on a regular basis.

Summary

If your team has a clear sense of purpose and direction you will recognise this in their motivation, energy and enthusiasm. Your role as a team coach is to facilitate the team to develop that purpose, and identify the goals, roles and activities needed to achieve it. This will involve you in bringing out the best in the team, encouraging them to share expertise, collaborate together and develop the confidence to take on new challenges. Use the results of the questionnaire at the beginning of this chapter and the ideas presented in this chapter to identify some actions you can take to coach your team to develop greater clarity around their purpose, goals and roles.

Actions from this chapter

ACTION	TIME FRAME	TEAM IMPROVEMENT	REFLECTIONS AND PROGRESS REVIEW
1.			
2.			
3.			

Managing performance

Once your team has established their purpose, goals and roles, the challenge is to help to keep them on track so that they can achieve their goals and develop their performance.

This chapter will focus very much on the processes and frameworks you can set up to support and build the performance of the team and the individuals in it.

It will show you how to:

- understand the importance of managing team and individual performance
- deal with difficult performance issues
- build alignment and integrate the 'four Rs' of successful performance management
- understand how to implement performance management into your team coaching process.

The importance of good performance management

Performance management does not always have a good reputation. A survey of nearly 200 companies found that while almost all, 90%, carried out appraisals nearly four out of 10 managers considered these to be merely tick-box exercises[1]. Your challenge as a team coach is to reverse these statistics and integrate performance management successfully into the very heart of the team.

The team leaders who achieve this offer clear frameworks and set team objectives that are realistic as well as challenging. They are also comfortable dealing with mavericks, star performers and slow learners. No easy task! They sometimes have a touch of magic when it comes to helping their colleagues achieve their objectives. They provide great coaching support and are genuinely interested in developing others and seeing them grow. These types of managers are also great at talent spotting younger staff, or those who have been rather neglected, and enjoy helping them gain the confidence and skills they need. It's not unusual to hear that they have 'transformed' someone who previously had a hopeless reputation.

Managed well, good performance management can deliver some substantial bottom-line results and in addition it can also be a very satisfying process, helping the team and the individuals in it to grow and develop.

Insight

Here is what one manager has to say:

> Working in a large multinational organisation I have had the opportunity to develop three teams from scratch. Of course it's sad when people leave you to move on across the organisation to other opportunities, but it is also one of the most rewarding parts of my role. I'm really proud of what each of these teams has achieved and my role in helping to develop the people in them.

TAKE AWAY

Performance management can be one of the most satisfying and enjoyable aspects of your role.

To assess your approach to performance management, complete the following performance management audit. Also ask team members to complete it to provide feedback on how well the performance management process is working for them.

PLEASE SCORE ON A FIVE-POINT SCALE: 1 MEANS STRONGLY DISAGREE AND 5 MEANS STRONGLY AGREE		YOUR SCORE	COMMENTS
1	In my team we take performance management seriously.		
2	Individuals in the team have clearly defined objectives.		
3	The team goals and objectives are understood by all team members.		
4	Performance issues are dealt with in our team.		
5	The team meets together to review their progress on a regular basis.		
6	Team members receive regular feedback on their performance. **Note:** regular = at least every month		
	Total		

If you scored:

25 or above

You are managing the performance in your team well. Your team is clear about their expectations and understands what they need to do. By having regular reviews you can adapt to any changes, provide regular feedback, spot any performance issues and provide the support to keep everyone on track for success.

11–24

You are attempting to manage the performance in your team and whilst you are having some degree of success, there are improvements you could make. Look at the areas where you and the team have a low score and identify a plan to improve them over the next few months. Talk these through with team members so that you can get some idea of what they need to help them work more effectively.

0–10

In terms of performance management it is important that you start to set up some processes to help your team. Even if your organisation doesn't have an official system you can organise meetings to discuss objectives and progress and provide performance feedback. If people don't know what is expected of them, they won't know what to deliver.

Building alignment

One of the important aspects of performance management is that it aligns the objectives of the business with that of the team and the individual team members.

The objectives you and your team members set together should fit in with the organisation's goals, the overall team goals, and also reflect the individual's role and aspirations. The Building alignment model (see Figure 8.1) will help you and the team focus on the overall process and will also help to identify any individual or team development needs required to meet these objectives.

Figure 8.1 Building alignment model

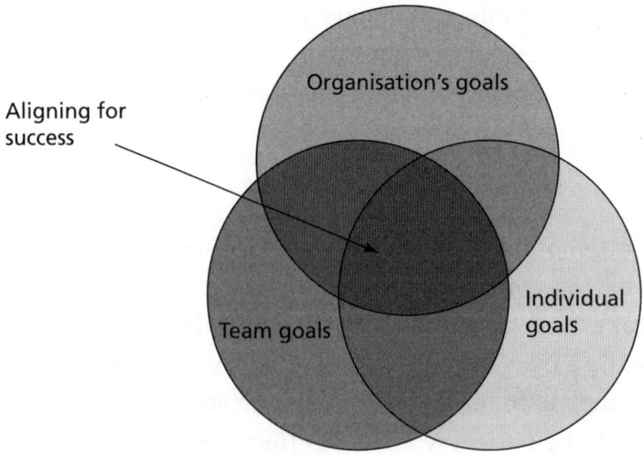

What are the goals of your organisation?

What are the goals of your team?

How does this fit into the goals and objectives of the individual team members?

The four Rs of successful performance management

When you set goals and objectives with your team it's important that they meet the criteria shown in Figure 8.2:

Figure 8.2 The four Rs of successful performance management

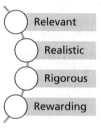

RELEVANT

Goals and objectives should fit firmly in the centre of the alignment diagram (Figure 8.1) and be relevant to the organisation and team success, and to the individual.

REALISTIC

It's important to make sure that any objectives are realistic, ambitious and achievable. If objectives are too easy, team members won't put in much effort; equally if they are impossible to achieve, people will give up. The challenge is to hit the sweet spot where the team will be stretched. Your role is to help identify the capabilities in the team and encourage members to work together to achieve success. If you set these objectives together rather than imposing them, you will have the buy-in and commitment of the team.

RIGOROUS

Performance management also requires rigour. Objectives need to be defined in terms of outcomes which can be measured. They also need to have clearly defined milestones and time scales. It is important to regularly review progress, celebrate progress and motivate the team to continue on the path you have set together. As a team coach you can provide encouragement and if performance slips, you can provide the feedback, coaching and development to keep everything on track.

REWARDING

People need to feel some sort of reward for their hard work. This does not always need to be financial but it is important that they feel some sort of motivation and satisfaction in what they do. Research shows that the top motivators for managers were[2]:

1 challenging and interesting work
2 the opportunity to learn and develop skills and knowledge
3 a high basic salary
4 autonomy
5 career advancement
6 knowing what I do has an impact.

You might like to reflect on this list with regard to your team. Try to link in with what motivates your team members so that they have the energy and enthusiasm to achieve their goals and objectives.

Implementing a performance management process for your team

Traditional performance management processes are based around a yearly cycle of objective setting, with quarterly or half-yearly reviews. We will see later in this chapter that many organisations are moving away from this process as it has become unwieldly and doesn't always reflect the fast-paced environment in which we work.

However, whatever processes your organisation uses, the success of any performance management rests on the quality of the conversations you have with your team.

It is very important to take time to plan the performance review conversations you want to have with your team members.

ONE-TO-ONE MEETINGS

Whilst your organisation may provide guidelines for when meetings should take place, you may need to take that initiative yourself and you should at least be aiming at quarterly reviews with team members.

There are three stages to the success of any performance management conversation (see Figure 8.3). These are the preparation you and your team do *before* the review, the quality *of the conversation you have* during the review and the action steps and follow-up *after* the review.

Figure 8.3 The three stages of a successful performance review

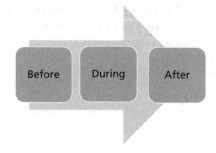

Before · During · After

Here are some suggestions which can help the process work smoothly:

Before the review

Prepare	You both need to spend time preparing for the meeting. Be clear about what you want to get from the conversation.
Use a range of data	Collecting views from customers and colleagues in other parts of the company may reveal hidden depths and insights about the individual that you may not be aware of.
Create the right environment	Book a meeting and make sure it is a private and neutral space where you can both talk freely. You will also be away from any interruptions.

During the review

Structure the discussion	Make sure the review stays on track, and summarise at regular points during the meeting. Ensure there is time to discuss development opportunities for the future. Use your coaching skills to build rapport, ask open questions and listen, so that you have a balanced conversation.
Provide balanced feedback	Use the SOFA feedback framework from Chapter 2 and remember to provide balanced feedback. Remember to be precise with your feedback. Research by CEB Corporate Leadership Council demonstrates that when managers focused on exploring performance weaknesses they saw performance decrease by 27%. However, when they focused on performance strengths they saw performance increase by 36%[3]. Also use the review as an opportunity to get some feedback on your role and how as a team you could improve and develop the way you work together.
Give your full attention	Give all your attention to the discussion and do not be distracted by interruptions, text messages, emails or thinking about your next meeting.

Provide support	Identify what support people need from you and the team. Make sure people have the skills, capabilities and resources they need to achieve their objectives.
Look to the future	You need to devote time to look at what has been achieved and also focus on what needs to be achieved in the coming months.
Agree next steps	Make sure that the objectives, approach and outputs are agreed. It's often helpful at the end of the meeting to let the other person summarise the key points.

After the review

Follow up	Keep a formal record of what's been discussed and what has been agreed going forward. Both of you should agree this.
Development plans	Along with agreeing and monitoring objectives, make sure that development plans are in place.
Set up review meetings	Set up the next review meeting and agree when this will be, so that you can review progress, provide support and adapt the objectives to any changes that may be taking place.
Provide regular feedback	Performance management is an ongoing process so make sure you provide regular feedback throughout the year. There should be no surprises at a performance review – anyone who is underperforming should already know about the issues.

Insight

Here is what one manager has to say:

Prior to our performance review I asked a new team member to fill in a self-evaluation form. He rated his skills and experience at a much higher level than I had. I was concerned about how I could address this issue without

▶

demotivating him. I gave it a lot of thought and developed some clear examples of what my expectations were and what was involved to meet and exceed these expectations.

During the meeting I started out with the things I thought he did well and let him know that these were on target and that I appreciated him. I then moved on to the areas where there were gaps. I explained the expectations by giving examples and also explained what was needed to exceed these. I paused frequently and gave him the opportunity to respond. At the end of the meeting he made a comment that I was the first manager who had actually told him what he needed to do to be better at his job. This surprised me but also made me realise that the conversation had been constructive and we had also maintained a positive working relationship.

TAKE AWAY

Plan for your conversation and provide clear feedback. Be clear about the expectations and standards for the role.

New approaches to performance management

Many organisations are finding that the traditional approach to performance management isn't working for them. In a VUCA* world they need a process which is more agile and flexible and able to adapt to change. In addition there is a recognition that employees want a more individualised approach and one which helps them to work to their strengths.

When Deloitte[4] reviewed their traditional approach to managing performance they found that 58% of executives believed that the current approach 'drives neither employee engagement nor high performance' (and it was consuming 2 million hours a year!).

As they researched further they discovered that in their highest-performing teams, team leaders conducted regular check-ins with each team member on a weekly basis. As they put it: 'very frequent check-ins are a team leader's

*VUCA = volatile, uncertain, complex and ambiguous

'killer App'.' Rather than a long, drawn-out, review process they now capture a 'performance snapshot' which can easily be collated and reviewed to identify development needs and succession plans.

They also found that another defining characteristic of their best teams was that team members felt that they were working to their strengths and doing what they do best every day.

These findings are backed up by the experience in other organisations. At Atlasian, the Australian software company[5], managers replaced their traditional performance management approach with a more lightweight continuous model, using their weekly one-to-one meetings as an opportunity for feedback and coaching. These meetings focused on how individuals could enhance their performance and play to their strengths.

As well as greater emphasis on ongoing feedback and building on strengths, the organisations that are updating their approach to performance management are asking more person-centred questions. They are also involving other colleagues in the review process to create greater transparency.

Google[6] operates a peer review process where the individual and their manager nominates a group of peers (including some who are more junior to them) and asks them the following question:

> List one thing this person should do more of and one thing they should do differently to have a greater impact on the company.

These newer approaches to performance management are certainly providing a more agile, flexible and immediate way of directly working with employees to help them manage their performance and development. However, they require managers to have the skills to observe and recognise performance, to provide regular coaching and feedback, and help their people constantly develop and improve their performance: the skills of a great team coach. This may sound like more work for you, as team leader, but in the long run, shorter and more focused conversations will enhance team performance.

Team performance reviews

Often, performance management is dealt with on an individual basis, even though people rarely work in isolation. An individual's success is usually the result of the support and input from other colleagues and team members.

As a result it is equally important that you meet together to review the overall team performance, on a regular basis. These meetings should not be just a review of the targets, revenue and budget projections. You need to reflect on the way the team is working together to achieve these goals. This means going back to the team goals you set, and reviewing your team charter to look at:

- What is working well for us?
- What success have we had?
- Is there anything we need to change?
- How can we support each other?
- What can we do to build on and improve performance in the team?
- What support do you need from me?

Use these meetings as a chance to celebrate success and give each team member the opportunity to share what they are doing, and provide an update of where they are with their contribution to the overall team goals.

Top tips

- Regard performance management as a regular, ongoing process rather than a one-off event.
- Link individual goals to organisational and team goals.
- Focus on the positives and build on strengths.
- Understand the aspirations and development needs of team members.
- Ensure that performance management is not just one-way: a process which includes upward, peer and customer feedback will provide more valuable data.
- Build in time to review your performance as a team.

Summary

Building the performance of the team not only helps to achieve the overall goals and targets, but it has the potential to supercharge your team and help them to work more effectively together.

In this chapter we have provided an overview to help you think about how to structure your approach and create the processes and frameworks which can help the team to grow.

Identify some ideas and action you and your team can put into practice to build performance.

Actions from this chapter

ACTION	TIME FRAME	TEAM INVOLVEMENT	REFLECTIONS AND PROGRESS REVIEW
1.			
2.			
3.			

Collaborating with others

For any team to achieve its goals and objectives it needs the support of other teams. These may be colleagues and departments in the organisation or may also involve external partners based in different locations. Collaboration is all about how your team interacts with the various stakeholders who are important to the overall success of the team. This chapter provides an overview of collaboration, and will help you to transform and improve how your team works with others. As the seventeenth-century poet John Donne said, 'no man is an island', and the same concept applies to teams.

This chapter will help you to:

- understand the power of collaboration and why it can be a game-changer for your team
- assess how well you and your team currently perform in terms of collaboration and managing beyond the boundaries of your team
- develop a range of techniques and approaches to improve collaboration.

The power of collaboration

First, let's reflect on the power of collaboration. Recent research at MIT using electronic data-collecting badges has made it possible to accurately map team activity and communication. The research found a strong link between collaboration and business success. Creating a more collaborative environment in a call centre, just through the introduction of a common team coffee break, led to an overall 8% increase in performance (and in fact created a 20% increase in performance for the worse-performing areas).

Equally, when working with a major German bank on a product launch, researchers found that there was uneven communication between the four teams, with the customer service team almost totally ignored in the communication process. They also identified an over-reliance on one form of communication – email. It was only when the project was heading for failure that all the teams began to communicate and met to work out how to proceed together[1].

These examples both illustrate that collaboration is more important than ever, and the more complex the project you are working on, the greater the need to collaborate with others.

What does good collaboration look like?

Think back to a time when your team has benefited from good collaboration. What happened and what made it successful?

Also think of a time when collaboration didn't work. What went wrong and what got in the way?

The list below may well describe your experiences.

CHARACTERISTICS OF POOR COLLABORATION	CHARACTERISTICS OF GREAT COLLABORATION
• A competitive mindset • An atmosphere of blame, over-promising and under-delivering • Intransigence • Lack of trust • Difficult issues are ignored or discussed superficially • Poor communication • Lack of accountability and agreement on time scales • Lack of empathy with others • Language problems • If plans are set, they are broken regularly • The goalposts are continually moving – often creating more complexity or wasting existing work already completed	• A great mindset of win/win • Trust • Willingness to be flexible and compromise • Shared responsibility • Partnership ethos • Clear communication using a variety of channels • Accountability • Clear plan of work, deliverables and key review stages • Common (shared) goals • Agreed plans are rarely, if ever, broken except in times of crisis • Honesty and truth-telling to each other • Respect • Conflict resolution skills (openly discussed)

The characteristics of good collaboration can be pulled together into four key principles – VACE (see Figure 9.1) – and these are explained below:

- Values
- Approach
- Communication
- Empathy.

Figure 9.1 Characteristics of good team collaboration

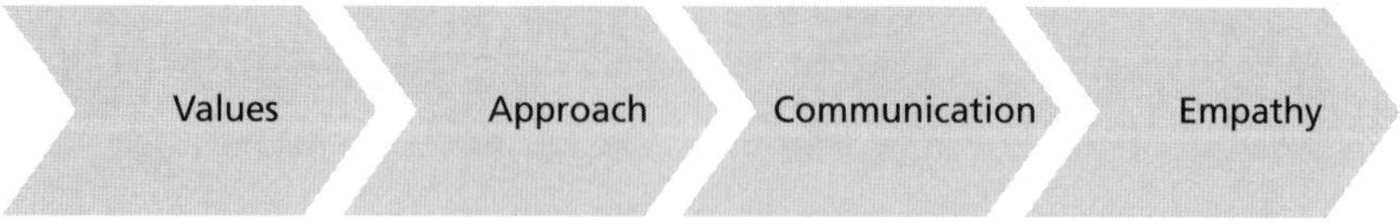

Values Approach Communication Empathy

- **Values.** Collaboration requires a willingness to see the other person's point of view and understand what is important for them. For it to work effectively there needs to be a degree of trust and respect – this can only happen if people understand and share some common values around the area they are collaborating on.

- **Approach.** It also requires a planned approach so that people know when and how to collaborate. This process doesn't happen by accident and needs the commitment of everyone involved and an agreement on how they will all work together.

- **Communications rich.** Part of the planning should focus on the nature of the communication. What do you need to communicate and what is the best format to use? Regularly reviewing the communication process will help everyone to stay on track. One radical change at Coca-Cola recently is a ban on voicemail messages which can be an inefficient way of sharing information.

- **Empathy and people skills.** Empathy and an interest in building good personal relationships is key, but it is equally important to negotiate and challenge when appropriate. The MIT research referred to earlier highlighted that in successful team collaboration, all team members talk and listen in equal amounts and connect directly with each other on a regular basis.

Consider the principles shown above and think about how much of this is reflected in the way your team collaborates with others.

Insight

One of the team leaders we interviewed highlighted the power of empathy:

Some team leaders just focus on getting the job done and don't realise what a difference a positive attitude and understanding of others can make. It helps people to relate better to other people across the rest of the organisation. You need to have the right attitude, and a positive mindset, in order to create successful collaboration.

TAKE AWAY

Good collaboration requires empathy and focus on people.

Think about the following statements in the collaboration audit and ask everyone in the team to complete these ahead of a team discussion.

PLEASE SCORE ON A FIVE-POINT SCALE: 1 MEANS STRONGLY DISAGREE AND 5 MEANS STRONGLY AGREE		
	YOUR SCORE	COMMENTS
As a team we have identified a list of key people/ departments/ business areas we want to collaborate with.		
I understand the value of managing across boundaries in the organisation.		
We are respected in terms of how well we collaborate in the organisation.		
We regularly spend time considering how to improve collaboration with others across the organisation.		
We hold regular planning meetings with others who we collaborate with.		
My organisation has a culture that encourages collaboration between different teams/business areas.		
Total		

If you scored:

25 or above

Your team clearly appreciates the importance of collaboration and already has a good reputation across the organisation. You may want to check out how your stakeholders experience working with the team and consider what else you can do to enhance and maintain your relationships.

11–24

Your team is working on some aspects of collaboration. Look at the areas where you scored low. What can you do to improve these scores and enhance your level of collaboration? Some of the exercises later in this chapter will help you to reflect on your collaboration challenge.

0–10

Your team has not grasped just how valuable collaboration is. Perhaps you also lack the time or resources to review and improve what you currently do. Work with your team to identify your key stakeholders and build the networks and relationships key to your success.

Insight

One team leader realised that her team needed more awareness about all the different departments they needed to collaborate with.

As many of the team members were new, she set them the challenge of mapping all their contacts. Each team member did this individually and then together they drew up a team collaboration map:

It's really important that the team knows who to go to. Many of them have built positive relationships and understand the constraints their colleagues face.

I always make sure that if other departments and teams provide a great service we say thank you to show how much we appreciate their support.

TAKE AWAY

Recognise, develop relationships, and provide positive feedback to the people and teams you collaborate with.

Try this

Who do you need to collaborate with?

Think about the key relationships outside your team which are important to the success of your team. These may be both internal and external to the organisation. Select the five most important relationships, and think about:

- how important the relationship is to your team; and
- how effective the relationship is at the moment.

NAME OF COLLABORATION PARTNER	IMPORTANCE OF THE RELATIONSHIP ON A SCORE OF 1–10	QUALITY OF THE RELATIONSHIP ON A SCORE OF 1–10
1.		
2.		
3.		
4.		
5.		

You may prefer to map your stakeholders onto Figure 9.2. This will clearly show you, and your team, whether the quality and the importance of the relationship are closely aligned.

Figure 9.2 Mapping your relationships

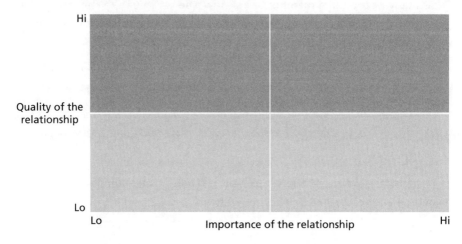

Of course the ideal place for your key collaboration partners is the top right-hand box. However, as well as your own analysis, it is best to go out to your stakeholders and find out what they really think. You can also discuss how you can improve the relationship, so that you can work together more effectively.

MAPPING TOOLS

Another way of mapping your stakeholders is to work with your team to build up a map or spider diagram (see Figure 9.3) of all the stakeholders you have. To do this:

- Take a sheet of flipchart paper. In the centre draw a circle to represent your team or the project you are working on.
- Add lines for each of the people/teams you collaborate with. You can get creative here:
  - Use thick lines to represent good relationships, dotted lines where the relationship is weak and more jagged lines if you have conflicting relations.

- Use different colours to represent different locations or partners from outside the organisation.
- You can also add +++ signs to indicate the importance of the relationship to the team.

Figure 9.3   A team stakeholder map

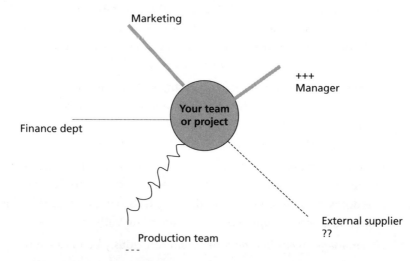

Once you have the relationships mapped you can then work out your collaboration strategy:

- What actions can you take to build the good relationships and improve the weaker relationships?
- Which team members are best placed to build those relationships?
- Identify how you will build collaboration: should it be face-to-face, email, social networking, etc.?
- Are there other people who should be on the stakeholder map?
- If you have any relationships which are not positive, think about how important these are for the team's success and what you and others can do to improve the situation.

This exercise will give you and the team the opportunity to develop a collaboration strategy together. Remember to set up a time to review your progress and adapt the map to reflect any changes in the organisation that may impact on the team.

Ideas for collaborating

Many of the managers we interviewed had some interesting views and examples for building collaboration outside their teams. Some of these examples may be ones you could implement with your team:

- Set up an ideas exchange. One organisation hosted a company-wide series of '*Ideas Exchange*' events to look at how they dealt with key bottlenecks such as overcapacity, dealing with customer production changes and managing major holiday periods.

- Another manager asked the IT department to audit how well their current technology supported collaboration and identified a number of changes they could make. This is also something where the more internet-savvy members of the team could help out.

- Another manager we worked with linked into the organisation's Facebook page. He travelled a lot, so kept the team updated with anecdotes, pictures and team updates. This forum is now used by the team and by others who work and collaborate with each other.

- One manager described how her team consciously build relationships and networks. Each of them attends different forums and events in and outside the organisation as a way of not only building knowledge, but consciously building relationships.

Top tips

- Assess your networks and identify who you and your team need to collaborate with.

- Actively develop a collaboration strategy and share the responsibility in the team.

- Remember that collaboration is a two-way process. Think about what you can do to support others.

- Get feedback from your stakeholders and explore their issues and concerns. Be willing to walk a mile in their shoes!

- Always consider 'how can we work together to improve what we do?'

- Make sure you regularly review the collaboration process as people, teams, issues and priorities rarely stay the same for long.

Summary

As organisational life is becoming more complex, the need for collaboration is increasing and the benefits to organisations can be immense. Teams need to be more agile and versatile. We have provided an overview of what good collaboration looks like with some ideas, suggestions, top tips and techniques you can use to coach your team to develop their approach to building collaboration. Collaboration isn't complex, it just takes some conscious thought and effort to make it happen.

We asked the company secretary of a multinational what he considered as key to effective collaboration. After all, he had worked at board level for 20+ years, served on countless committees and action groups and seen any number of new generations of people progress up through the business:

> Collaboration? Well, essentially we are talking about cooperation and it all comes down to personalities.

Basically it comes down to developing good personal relationships – these are critical for you and your team.

Actions from this chapter

Identify the actions you and your team can take to build a culture of collaboration in your team and with those you work with.

ACTION	TIME FRAME	TEAM INVOLVEMENT	REFLECTIONS AND PROGRESS REVIEW
1.			
2.			
3.			

Working with change

Change is something of a constant in most people's lives and is likely to have a huge impact on the team. Whether it is a change in the team structure, ways of working or a complete reorganisation, we are constantly working with and reacting to change. The challenge that change brings can be seen as positive, bringing with it the chance to innovate and try new things. However it can also be associated with a sense of confusion, loss and instability.

As a team coach it is important that you are aware of the psychological impact of change on your team, and that you develop ways of building engagement for the future.

This chapter will help you to:

- understand more about how people experience change
- build engagement to change in your team
- coach the team to find ways of working effectively with change.

How people experience change

How your team members experience any change will depend on the change itself, the impact it will have on them (both real and perceived) and their personal appetite for change. A major reorganisation, merger, job losses or redundancies are major changes for people to deal with. There often may be a lack of clarity about the impact of the changes and the longer this goes on for, the harder it is for people to deal with the lack of certainty. Some of us enjoy change, most find it unsettling and uncomfortable.

When people experience change they follow a similar emotional reaction. We often refer to this as the change curve (see Figure 10.1), which has been adapted from the work of Elizabeth Kübler-Ross. People move through the change curve at different speeds and as a team coach it's important to be aware of how different members of your team experience this process.

Figure 10.1 The change curve

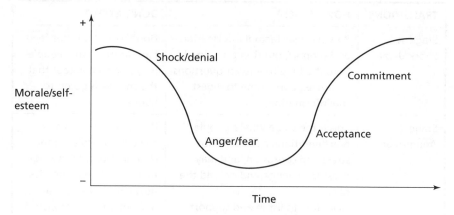

Source: Adapted from *On Death and Dying* by Dr Elisabeth Kübler-Ross, 1969, Scribner[1]

There are four key stages on the change curve. Shock and denial at the change: people won't have grasped what is happening and the impact on them. This is often followed by a period of anger and fear. During this time people will be expressing their anger and resistance to the change. They may be afraid of what it will mean for them. Over time the change will be accepted and eventually people will let go of the past and be more committed to new ways of working.

The change curve can be a useful tool to use as a team coach to help manage and support people through these transitions. Your support will also help to accelerate the change process by:

- minimising the negative effects of change
- recognising and working with any resistance to change
- understanding that people can't immediately move from shock to commitment
- supporting people through the process.

The table below will help you to understand what you can do to support your team through times of change, and also understand what you can't expect from them. Unfortunately, people rarely move straight from stage 1 to stage 4. All you can do is help them through the process as quickly as possible.

TRANSITIONS	HOW TO HELP	DON'T EXPECT
Stage 1: Shock/denial	Provide clear factual information and support, but don't overload. Take the time to answer questions and give people time to digest the information.	Don't expect a lot of feedback at this stage. People may not even accept that the change is going to happen.
Stage 2: Anger/fear	This is the stage where people react emotionally, experience stress and confusion, and may resist the change and defend the past. Give time to listen and support and provide people with space to work through the emotions they are feeling.	Don't expect everyone to be on board with the change. During this stage morale will be lower, sickness higher than usual and you may experience a drop in performance.
Stage 3: Acceptance	As people are gradually starting to accept the change, this is the time to explore new roles, and new ways of working. Listen, involve and build on their ideas. Set some short-term goals, provide training and reward new ways of working.	Don't over-expect. People will be tentatively trying out new ideas and may still hold on to the past.

▶

TRANSITIONS	HOW TO HELP	DON'T EXPECT
Stage 4: Commitment	This is a sign that people have accepted the new status quo. Make sure you celebrate achievements and provide feedback. People will be happy to take on more responsibility and show renewed enthusiasm.	Don't expect everyone to arrive at this stage at the same time – team members will be at different stages. Those that have arrived may be able to help others in the team to move forward.

Insight

One manager we worked with, who was leading a change project integrating a new system, realised how useful it is to recognise where individuals and teams are on the change curve.

Her team was very much on board with the change:

> . . . but other teams were much further behind and had some concerns about how things would work out in the future. We needed to think about the messages we sent out and varied what we said to take account of where people were. Some people needed reassurance, others were further ahead and wanted to get on with the change.

Interestingly, a year down the line the new system is the norm.

TAKE AWAY

Recognise that people are at different stages and tailor the way you communicate with others to reflect this.

Building engagement to change

Building engagement to change is very much a process of communication and involvement.

Here are 10 suggestions to help you and your team work through the process:

1 Communication is vital and you can never do enough of it. Your message needs to consistent, clear and positive. Try to build in stories about successes so that people can see progress and know that things are moving ahead.

2   Be authentic. Honesty is so important in times of change. Be clear about what is happening, and make sure you communicate a clear message and regularly update the team.

3   Allow people time to talk and express their views. It is important that people have a chance to talk, either on a one-to-one basis or with the team as a whole. However, you need to stay positive otherwise people will feel it's OK to complain and to opt out of the planned changes.

4   Help the team to get engaged in the change. Think about new roles and projects that they can become involved in and set some short-term goals and experiment with new ideas. The secret is to keep people moving and achieving, however small the progress.

5   Help to develop new skills and ensure that they have the training and resources for the future.

6   Manage expectations within the team and help people to develop confidence and find their way in the new environment.

7   Help people to be connected with the wider organisation not just through communication but through activities and events where they can come together to share ideas.

8   Be observant. Look for signs in the team of new energy and provide praise and encouragement.

9   Find time to speak with individual team members and gain a sense of how they are feeling and what you can do to support them. It can sometimes be helpful to pair up some of the more committed members of the team with those who are still struggling with the change.

10 Make sure you review progress on a regular basis, providing updates and information for the team, and celebrate success along the way so that people get a sense of achievement.

Insight

A hospitality director explained how they helped their team work through a major organisational change:

I had to make people believe they matter and show how their contribution impacts on the business. One significant change we made was to move from being a cost centre to a profit centre. This had a positive spin in that

▶

people now felt they were contributing to the business rather than being a drain on it. It helped to build confidence. I try and report the things that they can affect. If they know that smiling at customers wins business then they will smile more. It's important to tell a story that is meaningful to them and let them think on their feet. I want them to feel comfortable with ambiguity. This involves trusting them, letting them get on with it and being open to new ideas. We have regular meetings. In hospitality services the biggest customer touch point can be a stressful place to work, so we use fun and humour. Most people will get into the spirit of what you want to achieve if it is well communicated, and will go the extra mile themselves.

TAKE AWAY

Involve people in the change, and help them see the positive impact they can make.

CHANGE ASSESSMENT AUDIT

The questions below may be useful for you and the team to discuss and review your overall approach to working with change.

PLEASE SCORE ON A FIVE-POINT SCALE: 1 MEANS STRONGLY DISAGREE AND 5 MEANS STRONGLY AGREE		
	YOUR SCORE	COMMENTS
The team is involved in designing and implementing change.		
Team members have the opportunity to discuss their fears and concerns about change.		
Change is seen as a positive opportunity in this team.		
There is a clear vision for change in the team.		
There is good communication about change in the team.		
The team communicate well with external stakeholders and other teams who are impacted by the change.		
Total		

If you scored:

25 or above

You and the team have a positive attitude towards change. You talk openly together about your concerns and provide support to each other in order to understand and adapt to the changes you are facing. The team is also involved in planning and shaping how you implement and manage the change and is aware of the impact and involvement of stakeholders outside the team.

11–24

You and the team have made some progress on working effectively with change but there is still room for improvement. Discuss the comments and results from the questionnaire. Look at the areas where you all scored consistently highly and think about how you can build on this. Also look at the areas where you scored lower and work together, using some of the tools and techniques in this chapter to help you.

0–10

You have a lot to do in this area. As a team coach you need to understand the impact of change on others and support them through what can be a potentially challenging time.

Coaching your team through change and involving them in the process will mean that as a team you will be more effective and better able to anticipate the reaction of your stakeholders.

Working with your team

One of the secrets of working successfully with change is to build engagement and involvement. This takes time so don't expect everyone to immediately jump on board. Here are few ideas for team coaching activities you can work on with your team.

CREATE THE ENVIRONMENT FOR CHANGE

Build up a force field analysis of the situation with your team (see Figure 10.2).

Figure 10.2 Force field analysis

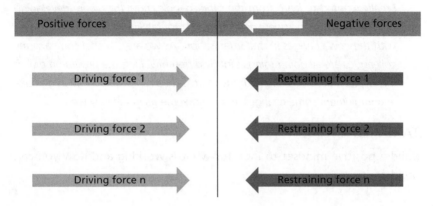

The idea of a force field analysis is to brainstorm all the negative forces and disadvantages about the change on one side of the chart and then brainstorm all the factors which are supporting the change. These may include the dissatisfaction with the current situation, the benefits and advantages of the change and the support to make it happen. You can use the length of the lines to illustrate the impact and importance of each force.

Once you have drawn up the force field analysis you can then look at how you can use the positive forces to overcome some of the restraining forces to help the team move ahead.

This is a good technique for airing people's views, building up the case for change and looking at how to practically move ahead.

USE THE PROCESS OF APPRECIATIVE INQUIRY

It's very easy to get pulled down into the problems and difficulties associated with change. Taking a more 'appreciative' approach can build energy and develop new ideas. The concept of appreciative enquiry was pioneered by David Cooperrider and his colleagues at Case Western Reserve University and is a process of looking for and focusing on real examples and stories of when things have gone well and using them to build a 'desired future', which you can work towards.

Ask your team to seek out and share positive stories and examples of change, exploring what worked, how it happened and what the effect was. You can use these stories and ideas to build up ideas and ways of working towards the end goal.

CONDUCT A CHANGE IMPACT ANALYSIS

This is something you can do with team members to reflect on what the change will mean for them. You can also use this as a tool to think about the stakeholders you are working with.

Stage 1

1   Identify the things you like that you will have to stop doing.

2   Identify the new areas that you will have to get involved with that you don't like.

3   Identify the things that will continue.

 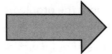

STOP	START	CONTINUE
Things I like	Things I don't like	

This is a good way of surfacing some of the feelings your team may have about the change. If you are doing this for your stakeholders it will help you to anticipate some of the negative reactions they may have to the change.

Stage 2

1   Identify the things you don't like that will stop.
2   Identify the new areas you can focus on that you feel positive about.
3   Identify the things that will continue.

 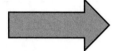

STOP	START	CONTINUE
Things I don't like	Things I like	

This stage helps you and the team to look at the positive aspects of change. If you do this exercise thinking about your stakeholders, it can help you think about how you present the change to others in order to identify some benefits and positive outcomes.

BUILD UP YOUR STAKEHOLDER MAP

In Chapter 9 we looked at the importance of building collaboration and understanding your stakeholders. Use the stakeholder mapping exercise in that chapter with your team.

Take each of the key stakeholders and think about:

1   What are their views about the change?
2   How are they feeling and reacting?
3   Where are they on the change curve?
4   How can they help or hinder the progress of the team?
5   Who do you need to target to help the team succeed?

6 Can you use some of the positive stakeholders to influence the stakeholders who are not positive about the change?

7 Are the people who are against the change important for the success for the team?

You can use this grid to map the stakeholders and identify who your supporters are, and who you might need to engage to deliver change successfully (see Figure 10.3).

Figure 10.3 Understanding your stakeholders

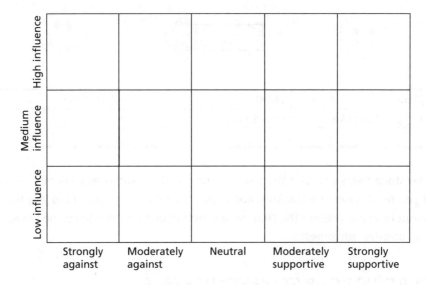

Top tips

- Try to understand the impact of change on your team members.
- Help people to move through the change curve.
- Communicate regularly with the team.
- Involve the team in implementing and planning the change.
- Make sure you identify and work with your key stakeholders.
- Your role and staying positive is important.

Summary

Change is very much a constant in our lives and this chapter has tried to highlight some of the issues your team may be facing. At the end of the day, for any organisation to change it is the people within it who have to change and your role is to make the journey a little easier for them. This takes time and patience.

Think about the changes your team is facing and identify some actions you could take to support and coach your team through the process.

Actions from this chapter

ACTION	TIME FRAME	TEAM INVOLVEMENT	REFLECTIONS AND PROGRESS REVIEW
1.			
2.			
3.			

Review: Focus on outcomes

The Focus on outcomes section provides you with some tools and techniques to develop a clear team purpose, and from that to clarify goals and roles for the team. It also helps you to reflect on the process and practice of managing team performance. Teams rarely work in isolation, so we have explored how you can work collaboratively with other stakeholders to achieve your goals. Finally, we have reflected on how to help the team work effectively through times of change, so that as a team you understand and support each other through the experience.

Figure 10.4 Focus on outcomes

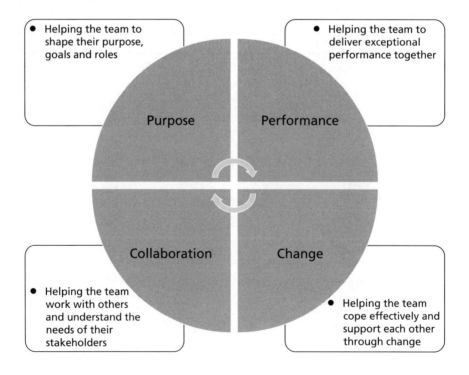

Progress review: Focus on outcomes

Use the questionnaire below to reflect on what you have taken away and applied from this section of the book.

Use a scale of 1–5 where:

1 = Never

2 = Rarely

3 = Sometimes

4 = Often

5 = Always

Circle your answer.

	YOUR ASSESSMENT 1 2 3 4 5
We have a clear, shared purpose in our team and everyone is aware of the goals we need to achieve.	1 2 3 4 5
Team members are aware of their roles and responsibilities.	1 2 3 4 5
We regularly review our performance as a team.	1 2 3 4 5
We align the organisation, team and individual goals together.	1 2 3 4 5
We collaborate well with other areas of the business.	1 2 3 4 5
We are aware of the needs of different stakeholders and actively manage them in the team.	1 2 3 4 5
I am aware of the impact of change on the team and on individual team members.	1 2 3 4 5
We work as a team to plan and implement changes together.	1 2 3 4 5

Review: Focus on outcomes

What have been the most important messages, skills or ideas that you have taken away?

How have you been able to apply this learning with your team and what results have you seen?

LEARNING	HOW HAVE YOU APPLIED THIS?	WHAT WAS THE RESULT?

Are there any aspects from the Focus on outcomes section that you need to refer back to for your own development?

Remember to refer back and dip into the different chapters for ideas and suggestions which you and the team can use together.

Focus on people

Focusing on the people in your team is essential. The combination of their skills, personalities and the way they interact and work together are central to the overall success.

> *The strength of the team is each individual member. The strength of each member is the team.*
>
> **PHIL JACKSON**, one of America's greatest basketball sports coaches

Your role as a team coach is to work with the individuals in your team to understand and bring out the best in them. In addition it is important to work together with your team so that the combination of all their strengths and talents can be used to complement and build a high-performing team, capable of riding the waves of change and delivering great results.

We have identified four key elements which make up the core of Focus on people. These elements can work to transform your team from a collection of individuals to a high-flying team who can ultimately support and coach each other.

This section will help you to understand how to engage and motivate both the individuals in your team and the team as whole. It will then go on to explore how to build the resilience levels in your team, and create a climate of trust both within the team and with the wider organisation. Finally, it will focus on building the potential of each team member so that together you can achieve your goals and ensure that as a team you are well prepared for the future.

Figure 10.5 Focus on people

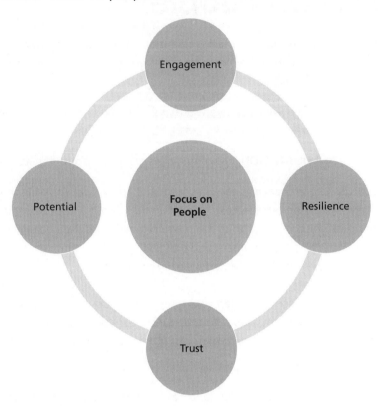

Building engagement

Building engagement and motivation has been shown to enhance performance. Research demonstrates that if people are engaged they will be delivering higher levels of productivity and customer service. Engagement has also been associated with increased creativity, reduced absenteeism and improved retention rates; so this really can be a game-changer for your team and the wider organisation.

This chapter will allow you:

- to understand the power of engagement
- to develop and harness the motivation and engagement in team members
- to build engagement in the team as a whole.

Motivation and engagement

There is a lot of debate around what we mean by engagement and how it differs from motivation. It's worth understanding these differences as both concepts are important for you as a team leader and coach.

MOTIVATION

Motivation refers to what drives and inspires individuals to put in discretionary effort and energy into their work. We often talk about extrinsic and intrinsic motivators. Extrinsic motivators focus on rewards such as money and bonuses, whilst the intrinsic ones are more internal to the individual. These focus on areas such as achievement, satisfaction, autonomy and responsibility.

Many organisations emphasise the extrinsic factors, yet Ashridge research asking 839 managers what motivates them illustrates just how important the intrinsic factors are (see Table 11.1).

The results indicate that if people have a good average salary, bonuses and incentives are not as important. Indeed there is plenty of evidence that incentives can have a negative effect on motivation, often focusing on short-term gains, and driving specific behaviours which are detrimental to team work and creativity.

Table 11.1 What motivates managers: the Ashridge Management Index (2008)

WHAT MANAGERS WANT (RANKING)		WHAT ORGANISA-TIONS RELY ON (RANKING)
1	Challenging/interesting work	2
2	Opportunity to continually learn and develop skills and knowledge	5
3	A high basic salary	6
4	Having the authority to 'run my own show'	15
5	Clear career advancement within the organisation	8
6	Knowing my decisions have an impact on the organisation	14
7	Performance-related pay/incentive schemes	1

Source: Ashridge Management Index 2008[1]

This is good news for you as the intrinsic motivators are the factors which you can help to influence.

ENGAGEMENT

Engagement goes a step further, as it is not just concerned with the individual but with the team and organisation. Engaged team members are committed and aligned to the goals and aims of the organisation. They care about the future of their company and are willing to invest discretionary effort to help the organisation succeed. There is plenty of evidence that this impacts on a whole range of metrics, as illustrated in Figure 11.1.

Figure 11.1 Adapted from the Benefits of Engagement

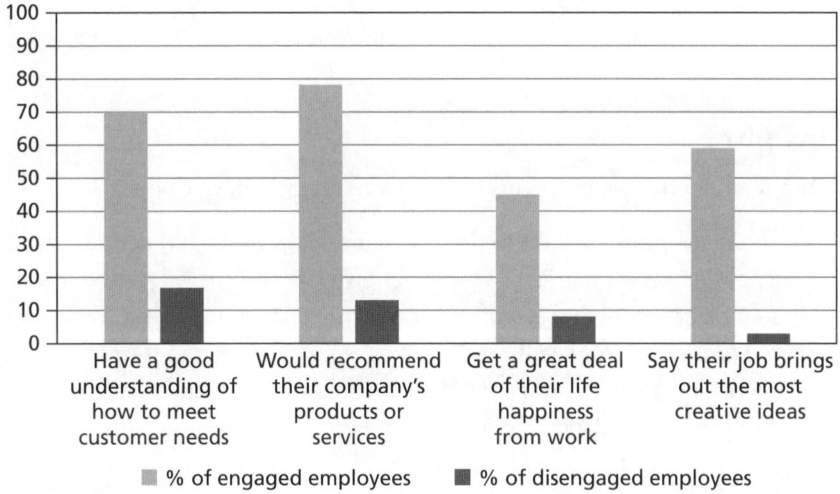

Source: George, M., 2013, steps to creating employee engagement[2]

As a team leader you need to coach both the individuals in your team and the team as a whole to develop their personal motivation and build commitment to the overall goals of the team and organisation.

Think about your team members and identify where they fit on Figure 11.2. Are they engaged and motivated or lost and switched off?

Figure 11.2 The link between motivation and engagement

Insight

One team leader we met worked with a team of IT developers:

The team are all very motivated. They are always trying to develop new ideas and keen to develop and learn new skills. My challenge is to make sure that everything they do is focused on the projects we need to deliver to our clients. This means creating engagement around the team purpose and also tapping into the talents and interests in the team to ensure that we spend the development time wisely.

TAKE AWAY

As a team leader you need to build both motivation and engagement to make sure everyone is pulling in the same direction.

Understanding what motivates team members

The challenge of creating engagement in the team is not just building a clear direction that people can align with but also linking into the individual motivations of team members. This isn't difficult to do, it just requires you to think about your team members and understand a little bit about what enthuses them.

Next time you are with one of your team members ask them the following questions:

- What do you enjoy about your role?
- What is important to you regarding your role?
- What do you want from your work?
- What would it take to make you stay with an organisation?
- What would make the work environment a great place for you to work in?

These questions will give you some insight into what drives and motivates your team members. It can help you to think about how to develop their role and ensure that that they remain motivated and are able to develop and contribute fully to the team.

Another approach is to reflect on each of your team members and think about their preferences. In Chapter 4 we looked at the Head, Heart and Gut model.

Use Table 11.2 to think about the preferences of your team.

Table 11.2 Identifying the preferences and motivations of team members

HEAD	HEART	GUT
Agreed objectives	Communication	Focus on the task
Clear outcomes	Support and praise	Energy and drive
Time scales	Involvement of all	Sense of urgency
Defined responsibilities	Trust and respect	Hands-on approach
Logical ideas	Feeling that they have been listened to	Autonomy and freedom to succeed
Decisions based on fact and data	Open feedback	A challenge
An analytical approach	Enthusiasm and encouragement	Progress and achievement
Clearly defined processes and ways of working	Support	Clear outputs

Your **Head** team members will be motivated by a clear, logical approach and will get a real sense of satisfaction from being able to develop and work with a set of designed processes and frameworks.

Heart team members will be motivated by the involvement and relationships in the team. They will enjoy working with and helping others. They will also be motivated by encouragement and praise.

Finally, your **Gut** team members will be motivated by the opportunity to get on with the task and make progress. They will love a challenge and appreciate the freedom to achieve and focus on delivering results.

Once you have an insight into what motivates each of your team members, think about how to adjust your style and frame how you present ideas and opportunities to them in a way which will gain their commitment and buy-in.

Insight

One manager we worked with illustrated how he adapted his style to motivate individual team members:

> *The usual view is that a leader should treat everyone the same way but I believe now that a leader should adjust to people. I am learning to change my style so it better suits everyone around me.*
>
> *One of my team likes to drive things forward whilst the other is much more reflective. I try to give space to each of them so that they can work in a way which benefits the team but also works to their strengths.*

TAKE AWAY

Adapt your style so that you can link into the motivations of each of your team members.

10 ideas to help to build motivation in your team

1   Get to know your people, ask them what they enjoy about their work; don't assume you know.

2   Identify their strengths. If people are doing what they are good at they generally feel more motivated.

▶

3   Provide some stretch in people's roles so that they have some positive challenge. This is really important if people have a boring or repetitive job.

4   Small things can make a difference. Positive feedback and saying thanks can help to build motivation.

5   Involve people in creating the solution and help them to feel part of the process.

6   Listen and coach your team: your attention can have a positive impact on motivation.

7   Let the team know what is happening. Communicating results can create a feeling of ownership and belonging.

8   Find ways to monitor and measure progress; people like to feel they and the team are making progress. Make sure to reward success with the team on a regular basis.

9   Give people responsibility and freedom to achieve. This is much better than continually checking and micromanaging.

10 Focus on your own motivation: if you show a positive attitude, energy and personal motivation, it will pass on to the team.

Building engagement in the team

We have shown that whilst motivation is important, the combination of aligning this with team and organisational goals is the real game-changer. So what builds engagement (see Figure 11.3)?

Figure 11.3 Building engagement in the team

YOUR ROLE

Gallup research[3] has identified that there is a very clear cascade effect between leaders' and managers' engagement and that of their team. They found that managers who are directly supervised by highly engaged leadership teams are 39% more likely to be engaged than managers who are supervised by actively disengaged leadership teams. The link between engaged managers and engaged employees is even more powerful. Employees who are supervised by highly engaged managers are 59% more likely to be engaged than those supervised by actively disengaged managers.

So start by questioning and examining your own level of engagement and remember that how you behave will be amplified within the team. You are a role model.

KEEP THE PURPOSE AT THE FOREFRONT

Developing a clear purpose with the team is the cornerstone to building engagement. We looked at how to do this in Chapter 7. If everyone in the team knows what they are working towards they are much more likely to focus their time and efforts on achieving this. It is worth reviewing this at every team meeting, providing regular updates and celebrating successes along the way.

FOCUS ON AND DEVELOP STRENGTHS

In their book, *First Break All the Rules,* Buckingham and Coffman[4] illustrated that if people focus on 'what they do best every day,' and 'if they have the opportunity to learn and grow' they are more likely to be engaged. So spend some time working with the team to identify their strengths and set up a culture of continual development in your team. Remember, development does not just come from training programmes. It is a combination of learning from others, on the job training, and formal training. Think about ways in which you can encourage development in the team, such as:

- providing projects and assignments to build new skills
- pairing people up so that more experienced team members can coach others
- setting up a mentoring scheme so that team members receive mentoring and advice from other managers in the organisation
- creating a 10% rule, where team members have 10% of their time to work on new ideas or development initiatives

- encouraging and supporting team members to take up some self-development
- finally, ensuring that each team member has a development plan which is both tailored to their individual needs and dovetails into the overall goals of the team.

INVOLVE THE TEAM

Engagement is most powerful if you have the whole team involved, so build in time to explore these issues together. Ensure that team members share any new ideas and practices which can contribute to the team.

Also aim to create ownership around the team goals and facilitate a team discussion using some of the following questions:

- We need to achieve x by y. How can we achieve this together?
- What resources do we have in the team?
- How do we need to organise to achieve our goals?
- How can we support each other to achieve this?
- Is there anything we can learn from others?
- What ideas do you have to take this forward?
- What options do we have to achieve x?

Insight

One manager we talked to was passionate about engaging his team:

If we don't constantly come up with new approaches to meeting customer needs we won't survive. The whole organisation is keen on building involvement throughout the business. We have just started to implement some 'Let's talk' sessions between myself, my boss and team members from all different levels and grades. The monthly meetings are voluntary and gradually more people are joining in and taking part. I'm a great believer in communication. I try to get people to talk, to come and speak to me and make a point of communicating with everyone. We encourage people to come up with ideas and they do have some really good ones. We want it to be a good place to work, so people issues are really important. It's taken

▶

TAKE AWAY

Involve the team in making decisions and make time to communicate.

Use these questions to help you and your team reflect on their levels of engagement.

Table 11.3 Assessing the engagement levels in your team

PLEASE SCORE ON A FIVE-POINT SCALE: 1 MEANS STRONGLY DISAGREE AND 5 MEANS STRONGLY AGREE.		
	YOUR SCORE	**COMMENTS**
I have clear goals and objectives.		
I feel that I have the opportunity to develop my skills and expertise.		
I am aware of the overall aims of the team and the organisation.		
I have a high level of personal motivation for my job.		
I receive support from my boss and my colleagues.		
I feel I have the opportunity to contribute and make a difference.		

If the average overall score of all the questions is:

25 or above

Your team has a high level of engagement. It has a positive environment where team members are committed to the goals of the team and the organisation. Your challenge will be to work with the team to maintain and build on this success.

10–24

Your team has variable levels of engagement. Pay attention to the questions where team members scored lower. If there are some trends, work with the team to develop an action plan to build engagement.

0–9

Your team will not be working effectively. You will need to explore why the scores are low, and initially work with the team to create an overall purpose which they can buy into.

Top tips

- Coach people one-to-one to find out what motivates them, and where their motivation lies.
- Use the Head, Heart and Gut questionnaire to assess people's preferred style and flex yours accordingly.
- Build in plenty of challenges and opportunities for people to stretch themselves.
- Communicate regularly and involve the team.
- Offer regular praise and feedback, both support and challenge.

Summary

Developing motivation and engagement in your team requires you to get to know your team and understand their values and aspirations. We've tried to show this doesn't necessarily take a lot of time, but it does take the effort from you to be genuinely interested in your team. It is one area where time spent coaching both the individual team members and the whole team can reap immediate rewards.

Think about the actions you can take which will enhance and build the performance of your team.

Actions from this chapter

ACTION	TIME FRAME	TEAM INVOLVEMENT	REFLECTIONS AND PROGRESS REVIEW
1.			
2.			
3.			

Resilience-proofing your team

Resilience is the ability to recover from setbacks and to cope well with adversity. In the UK, 105 million days are lost each year as a result of workplace stress, costing employers £1.24 billion[1]. Whilst absenteeism and sickness can be easily measured, other symptoms, such as lower productivity, conflict, morale issues and customer complaints, are less quantifiable but have a serious impact on the organisation.

Building the resilience levels in your team can therefore be crucial for success Understanding and reacting to the signals of stress in yourself and others, and building a positive team environment, can go a long way to sustaining and building performance.

This chapter will help you:

- to recognise resilience in yourself and others
- to manage and build your personal resilience
- to develop a resilient team.

Resilience: how do you recognise it in yourself and in others?

Resilience, stress, well-being, 'bounce back', burn-out, toughness, mindfulness and emotional resilience are a few of the different terms used to describe how well you cope with life at work and also what happens to you at home.

We all have times in our lives when we are striving to achieve deadlines and working long hours. Equally, personal and family issues can have a huge impact on our resilience levels and productivity at work.

One of the tricky things about resilience is that we don't always recognise when our resources are being depleted until it's too late. Whilst stress can be positive, bringing extra energy and drive, it is rarely sustainable over time, and can lead to exhaustion and ultimately burn-out.

Here are a few myths and realities that people hold about resilience:

MYTHS	REALITY
If someone is determined and focused they won't suffer from stress.	Nobody is bulletproof when it comes to resilience. Even the most positive attitude won't save you if you continually overload your body and mind.
I will know when it's happening to me.	This is not always true as we often deceive ourselves and fail to notice the symptoms until it is too late.
A healthy diet and exercise will mean that stress can't harm me.	This will certainly help but it certainly won't prevent stress and burn-out.
It's easy to separate my work life from what happens at home.	You may think that you can control these two worlds but often the two collide; workplace stress and family worries can be a heavy burden that will follow you everywhere.
Only a few people suffer from stress.	The reality is that most people have suffered from stress at some stage in their career.

Everyone has a different level of stress tolerance and even within one person this can vary depending on the situation and how well resourced they are at the time.

REFLECTING ON YOURSELF

A good place to start thinking about resilience is to reflect on yourself:

- On a scale of 1–10 how resilient are you feeling at the moment?

  (1 being totally exhausted and 10 positive, confident, focused and full of energy.)

Thinking back over your own career:

- When have you felt really resilient? What was happening and what helped you to feel so resilient?
- When have you felt that your energy levels have been depleted? What was happening and what do you think caused the drop in resilience?
- What did you do to recover?
- What do you currently do to manage your energy and resilience?

As a team leader it is important to focus on this area of your overall leadership as your team will pick up and amplify any signs of stress you may be showing. Equally, if you are feeling under stress it will be having an impact on your health, your ability to work effectively with others and your overall mental processing and decision-making.

Here are some suggestions to manage your personal resilience:

Recognise your limitations	Make sure you have plenty of support
Build in some recovery time	Get a coach
Give yourself thinking time	Build a support network
Be aware of your behaviour and notice any changes	Focus on solutions, not problems
Get feedback from others	Have an interest outside work
Drink plenty of water	Look at your workload: focus on where you can add value and delegate the rest
Have a healthy diet	
Do some exercise	Learn to say NO
Take your holidays	Finally, BREATHE!
Turn your mobile and computer off at the weekend	

Looking at the suggestions, identify which ones you practise and which ones you can try over the next few months to build your resilience.

REFLECTING ON YOUR TEAM'S RESILIENCE

Your team members will have different levels of resilience, but do be aware that stress usually affects everyone at some time in their career so even the toughest team members can succumb.

Figure 12.1 shows some general signs of stress and burn-out. It is worth noticing and picking up on these issues with team members by checking out how everything is for them. It's also good to recognise them in yourself as these are all early warning signals that things are not right.

Figure 12.1 Signs of stress

Resilience is not often talked about at work. In some environments there is a reluctance to admit to feeling under pressure. Even to the point where someone is literally just about to fall over with stress, they will often pretend that everything is OK. As one manager pointed out:

If I say I feel depressed too often will my manager decide to get rid of me?

Why am I the only one to say I feel under pressure at work – I know others feel the same, as they say it privately but why won't they admit it at our team meetings?

We often notice that more experienced team leaders make the time to get to know their team members very well, so that any changes in mood or performance are detected early. Look out for things like irritability, and sudden, unexpected mood swings.

Thinking about your team members. Do you:

- know how your team members are feeling?
- know if there is anything outside work which could potentially deplete their resilience levels (new baby, bereavement, divorce, etc.)?
- recognise the impact of changes at work on the team?
- discuss how resilient people are feeling and how you and the team can support them?

Use the questions below to reflect on the resilience levels with your team.

PLEASE SCORE ON A FIVE-POINT SCALE: 1 MEANS STRONGLY DISAGREE AND 5 MEANS STRONGLY AGREE	
How well do we as a team deal with stress?	
Do we recover quickly from setbacks?	
How well do we manage in times of unexpected crisis, work overload or during sustained periods of change?	
How often do we talk about resilience and stress levels in our team?	
Does the team provide a positive and support-ive environment to work in?	
Is the overall work environment a positive and supportive one?	

Discuss these issues with the team, to explore:

- how resilient you feel as a team
- how you are coping with the workload
- what you can do to support each other.

It's also good to plan for the future. If you know you have a challenge looming in the future which could result in increased pressure and workload, try to work together to think about how you can plan, organise and share the responsibility together.

WHAT DO RESILIENT TEAMS LOOK LIKE?

Insight

Here is what one team leader had to say:

We have recently been through a tough change process and I do feel my team have been very resilient. However this didn't happen overnight.

I made a point of getting to know the team when I first came into the department and developed a strong senior leadership team. We are all visible. I also have an open-door policy so try to be available for people. In addition we make a point of building in an activity or lunch with our strategy meetings to help build relationships.

As a team we have been together for several years now and team members have gone through a lot of change and tough times, both in the business and in their private lives. Because of our strong relationships, and our willingness to talk about issues and challenges, we have been able to support each other through all the difficult times as well as continuing to perform well in our work.

TAKE AWAY

Good, supportive relationships and an openness to talk about challenges help the team to develop overall resilience.

A resilient team is one which has:

- a high degree of trust and openness
- team members who support each other
- a clear goal
- conflict that is handled well
- a social side to the team and it has fun.

Resilience-proofing your team

A 2009 campaign by Business in the Community identified four areas which can help to build emotional resilience. These are a good work environment, good relationships, good specialist support and physical health.

Building on this, here are a few ideas you could use with your team.

BUILD SELF- AND TEAM AWARENESS

It's important to understand your own reaction to stress. What are your trigger points and how do you know when you are moving from stress to distress?

Psychometrics such as the Myers-Briggs Type Indicator and the Strength Deployment Inventory[2] are a good way to help team members to understand each other better and understand each other's reactions to stress and pressure.

RECOGNISE THE LEVITY EFFECT

Levity is all about having fun and humour in the workplace. Just as stress produces adrenalin and cortisol, laughter produces serotonin and endorphins. As a result, levity has been linked to increased productivity and creativity. Some global organisations have taken this concept seriously, with Boeing identifying it as a competitive advantage, enhancing creativity and overall employee engagement[3]. This is supported by the CIPD employee attitude survey[4] which shows a clear correlation between high energy positive emotions and a range of performance indicators.

Figure 12.2 Relationships between emotions at work and key performance indicators

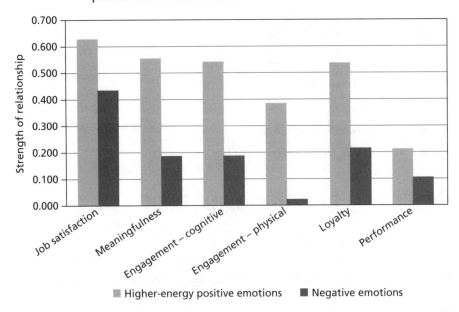

Source: CIPD Employee Attitude Survey 2006

TAKE BREAKS AND EAT LUNCH

Regular breaks have been shown to increase productivity and creativity, so build in a chance to go for a stretch and you will be able to concentrate for longer. In addition make sure you take a lunch break away from your desk as this will help you to recharge and boost your energy levels. Be aware of what you eat, and drink plenty of water. We all know what to avoid, and there are countless research studies to show that junk food and caffeine are not conducive to building resilience.

PROVIDE A SPACE TO TALK ABOUT ISSUES

One of the most important things you can do is to provide a listening ear to team members so that they can discuss their issues and challenges. Often, if you catch problems early on through coaching and support you can help the person handle the situation and prevent them moving into a more serious negative stress situation.

ENCOURAGE A HEALTHY LIFESTYLE IN THE TEAM

Try to encourage your team to make time for sport and exercise. Just taking a walk together can reduce some of the stress in the workplace. Also look at doing something as a team: training for a 5K run together or setting a team challenge, such as raising money for charity. These are all great ways of boosting morale as well as building resilience.

MANAGE THE ENVIRONMENT

Try to ensure that the work environment is one which allows people to focus on their work. Open-plan environments can be stressful for those who prefer peace and quiet to concentrate. Equally, working at home can be difficult for people who are extrovert by nature. Discussing these challenges and coming up with practical 'ways of working' as a team can help people to work more effectively together.

DO SOMETHING FUN TOGETHER

When you get together for a team meeting, build in something where you can all have fun together. This will help the levity factor and also help to build the relationships and trust levels in the team.

HELP THE TEAM TO TAKE CONTROL OF THEIR WORKLOAD

Stress often comes from feeling out of control, so help your team take control of their workload and prioritise the key tasks and milestones along the way. Be realistic in what can be achieved and try to get extra support if needed.

Plan for the work ahead and think about how people work together.

INVOLVE YOUR CUSTOMERS

When you are planning your workload and anticipating times when you think the team will be stretched, try to work with your customers so that you can even the workload out and ensure sufficient resources are available to meet the challenge ahead.

WORK-LIFE BALANCE IN THE TEAM

Help your team achieve a good work-life balance. There will be times when this isn't possible but make sure that overall the team achieves a good balance.

Also try to be flexible and allow people to flex their times to meet appointments and deal with family issues as they will generally repay you with extra support when you need it.

MINDFULNESS

Mindfulness is becoming a recognised concept in the workplace. It is the practice of being fully present and paying attention to the present moment without judgement. Many organisations are turning towards mindfulness training as a way of helping employees build their resilience, and manage the pace and stress of everyday life. It may be something that your team could benefit from and if you want to give it a go visit **www.headspace.com**[5] which will provide plenty of ideas to get started.

Insight

One manager faced a challenge when one of the team found that his son was seriously ill and would need an operation in the USA:

> *I realised that we, as a team, needed to provide as much practical and emotional support, as we could, so we helped to provide cover for the hospital appointments, and all joined forces to raise money through a half marathon. I hadn't realised that would have a powerful impact on the team. We trained together, some going as walkers, others as runners and others as supporters, and this in itself brought the team together. Even now, a year on, we are still doing lunch-time jogs, and I have noticed the general health and well-being of the team has improved.*

TAKE AWAY

Team support can go a long way to managing and supporting workplace stress.

Top tips

- Stress can happen to anyone at any time. Learn to spot the signs early, both in yourself and in your team.
- Make stress an open topic for discussion. If people feel safe to disclose it will be easier to support one another.
- Encourage the team to take regular breaks away from the desk.
- Try and incorporate occasional fun activities to help burn off stress.
- Behaviour breeds behaviour. Your team will follow your lead, so set a good example by ensuring you observe a healthy work-life balance as much as you can.

Summary

In this chapter we have looked at some of the consequences of stress and pressure on you as a team leader and also on the individuals in the team, recognising how important it is to know when people's energy levels are becoming depleted. We have also looked at the benefits of building a resilient team and identified some ideas for you and the team to focus on for the future.

Figure 12.3 provides a summary of the key resilience-building behaviours you can focus on together.

Remember, this isn't just your responsibility. Team members also have a responsibility to look after themselves, to communicate when the going is getting tough, and to support each other through difficult times.

Figure 12.3 A jigsaw of key resilience behaviours

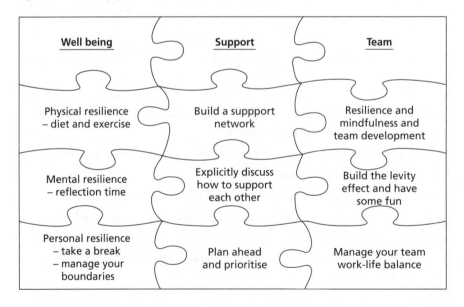

Actions from this chapter

ACTION	TIME FRAME	TEAM INVOLVEMENT	REFLECTIONS AND PROGRESS REVIEW
1.			
2.			
3.			

Developing trust

Trust is one of the most important ingredients for your team. Without it the team won't gel and won't be delivering results. Lencioni[1] has cited lack of trust as one of the five dysfunctions of an effective team, and there are countless studies relating trust to team and project performance, so this really is one element of team performance which cannot be ignored.

It is not only important to develop trust with your team members but also your stakeholders, clients or customers.

This chapter will explore what we mean by trust and how you can identify the levels of trust in your team. It will also help you to understand your role in encouraging and creating a trustful environment, and finally will provide you with some practical suggestions, top tips and ideas to build the trust within your team and the wider community.

This chapter will enable you to:

- assess the trust levels in your team
- understand your role in creating a high-trust team environment
- work as a team to generate the trust effect.

Assessing the trust levels in your team

Trust isn't always easy to define but we know when it is there, when it is absent and the effect this has on team performance.

> **Try this**
>
> Think about a team you have worked in with high levels of trust:
>
> - How did you work together and what were the results?
>
> Now think about a team with low levels of trust:
>
> - How did you work together and what were the results?

Below is a list of the possible effects of working in a low-trust environment. It's easy to see the impact this will have on performance:

- lower productivity
- ineffective problem-solving
- weaker team work
- more stress and socially generated uncertainty
- lack of quality information and costly checking systems
- lack of communication
- defensiveness
- doing the minimum
- feel compelled, not committed
- anxiety about other people's motives
- sensitive information withheld
- people needing proof
- people avoiding each other and protecting themselves
- people go where they can work freely with those they can trust.

Alternatively, a high-trust environment is one where there is:

- a high degree of openness
- respect for all team members
- sharing of ideas
- creativity and innovation
- regular communication
- feedback and praise
- a willingness to help each other
- a focus on collaboration
- an environment of high support and high challenge
- high morale.

Research by the Economist Intelligence Unit[2] highlighted the role of trust in meeting collaborative project goals. From a survey of 453 global business executives, 92% reported success in meeting their goals when they had complete trust in a key individual, as opposed to 45% when they had little trust (see Figure 13.1).

Figure 13.1 The role of trust

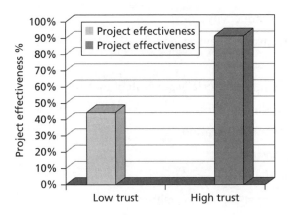

Trust in your team is something which develops over time. The questionnaire on the next page highlights some of the behaviours and attitudes associated with a high-trust environment and will help you and your team to assess your overall level of trust.

	Team members	YOUR SCORE	COMMENTS
	PLEASE SCORE ON A FIVE-POINT SCALE WHERE 1 MEANS STRONGLY DISAGREE AND 5 MEANS STRONGLY AGREE		
1	keep their promises and commitments		
2	share ideas openly and listen to others		
3	help each other out and recognise that they depend on each other to achieve the overall goal		
4	are honest and willing to admit mistakes		
5	give each other genuine praise and share credit for success with other team members		
6	include all the team members and value their strengths		
	Total		

If you scored:

21–30

Your scores indicate that you have a high level of trust. Reflect on what has led to these scores. You challenge will be to think about how to maintain and build on this as it really is an asset to your team. Remember that it will take time for new members of the team to build similar levels of trust.

11–20

There is some trust in the team. It will be useful to reflect on whether there were some questions which were more highly scored than others as this will help you to think about where to focus your energy in the process of developing trust.

5–10

You probably have a pretty low level of trust in the team. It will be worth thinking about why this has happened and, importantly, what steps you can take to start to build trust amongst people in the team. The ideas in the next two sections of this chapter will help you to start this process.

Your role in creating trust

As a manager, your role both as a coach and a role model is important in setting the tone for the team. Think about your approach and look at the descriptions below to identify which is most like you:

- Do you sometimes have a tendency to micromanage? Are you quick to make opinions about people in the team? Do you have high standards and find it hard to delegate? Do you focus on achieving the task at the expense of the relational side of managing your team?

- Do you feel that you trust others and are happy to give them a free hand? If they make mistakes, will you give them another chance? Is your attitude one which recognises that team members are adults so don't need too much guidance? Are you very open with your team, do you share information and are you happy to work with most people?

- Do you like to set clear accountabilities and objectives for your team members and provide them with the freedom to achieve their goals? Do you regard yourself as someone who is fair, but can be tough if you recognise that there are performance issues? Are you there to listen to problems and coach your team when needed?

Creating a trusting environment in your team is very much influenced by your leadership approach. If you are too controlling and task focused this can lead to an environment of mistrust and fear. On the other hand, if you are too trusting and don't set expectations, people will not have a framework in which to operate. There seems to be a healthy middle ground in creating a trusting relationship with your team which combines the freedom to make decisions and take initiatives with a clear set of boundaries.

Insight

One team leader we met discussed her approach to building an environment of trust in her team:

> *I don't micromanage, but I always give feedback and if I notice there is a problem I tackle it. I have regular one-to-ones with my team. What we talk about in these meetings is 100% confidential, and I feel that the team can*

▶

come to me to talk about most things. I see trust as a ripple effect. If I show trust to others, it is reciprocated and also develops across the team. I also encourage team members to help each other out, and now this is just part of our ways of working. We trust each other to say when we need help and to support each other. Finally, I've tried to help team members to be more open and understand each other. We have completed a couple of psychometric questionnaires and this has helped the team to be aware of each other's strengths and qualities.

TAKE AWAY

It's important to balance trust and accountability. Trust is also reciprocal and the team will mirror your behaviour and approach.

The skills and attitudes highlighted in the example above clearly demonstrate coaching behaviours which are important in creating an environment of trust:

- openness
- accountability
- setting boundaries through clear expectations and objectives
- willing to tackle tough issues
- listening and relational skills
- regular communication
- mirroring the behaviour you want to see
- giving trust to others.

Trust has to be earned, and it is ultimately in the eye of the beholder. For you to be trusted, others must perceive you are trustworthy. We often talk about trust being associated with credibility, competence, honesty and integrity, fairness, reliability and a clear positive intent.

Ashridge research[3] with the Clipper Round the World Yacht Race participants found some interesting insights into trust from the perspectives of the skippers and their crew. The crew described how they started from a positon of trust in the skipper, as the person in charge of the boat and their safety. If this trust was then damaged it became difficult for the skipper to influence and shape performance. On the other hand, the skippers started from a position of healthy distrust, as they had to gauge what each crew member was capable of. It was in the skipper's interest to develop their trust in the crew to allow them to step back with confidence and focus on the overall race performance and strategy.

The message from this is to be aware of others' expectations of you in terms of trust. What do you want from your team and stakeholders to demonstrate a relationship of trust, and what do they need from you?

Insight

One manager who was responsible for the project management of a huge IT infrastructure project described her role in building trust:

> My team knew I had their backs covered. We were working on a major change project and I provided a safety net for them. If any of the stakeholders were giving the team a hard time I'd sit down with the stakeholder and listen to their issues, and would back the team up. Obviously, if there was a legitimate problem I'd handle that with the team. However, I appreciated that they were all trying their best under tough conditions. On other occasions, such as difficult presentations or meetings, I'd make sure that I could be there to support the team member if they needed me. Ultimately the team knew they could rely on me.

TAKE AWAY
Trust needs to be earned and demonstrated.

Here are some suggestions to help to coach and build trust with your team:

1 BUILD SOCIAL CONNECTIONS AND UNDERSTANDING

Working in diverse teams can often create misunderstandings which can affect the trust levels in the team. Look for ways to increase the understanding amongst people. This may include completing a psychometric questionnaire together, getting to know more about each other, discussing cultural differences and customs. Trust is a key relational skill so time spent on this is certainly not wasted.

2 BUILD TRUST WITH YOUR STAKEHOLDERS

Trust within the team is important, but it is equally important to build the trust with your stakeholders and partners. One team leader consciously encouraged her team to go out and have a coffee with their stakeholders to build understanding. Again, if the relationship is solid it is easier to build trust and discuss difficult issues.

3 KEEP COMMUNICATING

One thing that has clearly come through all our conversations with team leaders and team members is the importance of dialogue. Regular communication, one-to-ones, team meetings and emails are all important. This is especially so in times of change, when trust can easily be eroded. As one team leader said: 'I try and give as much information as I can. It's important to be honest and provide support in order to maintain trust.'

4 BUDDY UP

Setting up a buddy system in the team can really help to build trust. In addition, mentoring and shadowing each other's jobs can enable people to appreciate and understand each other's roles. It also creates an expectation of mutual support so that team members can back each other up and provide assistance when needed.

5 REMEMBER, TRUST IS RECIPROCAL

As a team and with other teams, it is important to remember that trust is reciprocal. If you trust and support your colleagues, the likelihood is that they will do the same. Teams need to mirror this behaviour both in the team and outside to demonstrate their credibility and reliability.

6 CREATE TRUSTFUL WAYS OF WORKING

Working out how to create a trusting environment is best done as a team. Discuss some of the challenges you face as a team and create and agree some ways of working together. One virtual team we worked with had a challenge over team members answering emails. To handle this they agreed as a team that all emails should be answered within 24 hours. This meant that team members knew that they could rely on and trust their colleagues to get back to them. It is sometimes the simple things that can create and erode trust in the team and it's always best to discuss them early, before they become a problem.

7 CREATE AN ENVIRONMENT OF SUPPORT AND CHALLENGE IN THE TEAM

Finally, to develop trust in the team there needs to be openness and a willingness to not only support each other but also to challenge the way the team is working.

Try this

Looking at Figure 13.2, where would you place your team in order to create an environment of high support and high challenge?

Here are some suggestions to help you move into the high support/high challenge quadrant:

- Encourage people to come up with ideas to improve the team.
- Create an environment where people are keen to look at what is going well as a team and what could be improved.
- Be willing to listen to others.
- Be willing to challenge if there are things that you and the team are concerned about.
- Make sure as a team you spend time building the relationships and understanding which makes it possible to challenge and support in a positive way.

Figure 13.2 Creating challenge and support

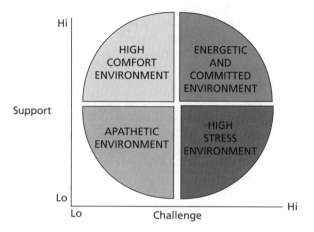

Top tips

- Resist the urge to micromanage. Try to trust your team to get on with the job.

- Trust is reciprocal so remember to show trust in others and give them the opportunity to develop and learn.

- Encourage the team to develop deeper relationships with key stakeholders.

- Trust is something with develops over time, so continually work to create a trusting environment in the team.

Summary

Trust in itself will not create the winning team or the game-changing result, but what trust does is to set up the environment for success. It will help your team to work more effectively both together and with your external stakeholders.

Coaching your team to develop their levels of trust requires you to initially reflect on your approach to trust and then to work with the team to encourage them to create the environment where the trust effect can flourish.

Actions from this chapter

ACTION	TIME FRAME	TEAM INVOLVEMENT	REFLECTIONS AND PROGRESS REVIEW
1.			
2.			
3.			

Developing team potential

Whether we have the opportunity to recruit the team we work with, or inherit an established team, we face the challenge of helping them to work together to perform both as individuals and as a team. In addition, given our constantly changing environment, with new systems, work processes and ever increasing workloads, it is important that your team stays abreast of changes and has the capability of managing any challenges that may be on the horizon.

In a recent McKinsey global research project, 'Building Capabilities for Performance'[1], half the respondents reported capability building as one of their top three priorities for this year, citing customer demand and strategic imperatives as key factors driving the demand for improved capabilities.

It is much easier to develop and retain existing talent rather than constantly bringing in new people. In addition, development activities also have the added benefit of increasing engagement, productivity and retention, as employees see that their organisation has a vested interest in them.

This chapter will help you to reflect on your team, understand their development needs and create a framework both for the individuals and the team as a whole to excel.

This chapter will support you in:

- identifying and managing the talent in your team from poor performers to rising stars
- thinking creatively about development opportunities for the team
- creating personalised individual and team development plans fit for the future.

Identifying and recognising the talent in your team

Think about your team members. They will all be different, with unique skills, personalities, and development needs. In addition they all have the potential to grow and improve their performance.

You can use the five Ps of performance and potential (see Figure 14.1) to help focus on your team.

Figure 14.1 The five Ps of performance and potential

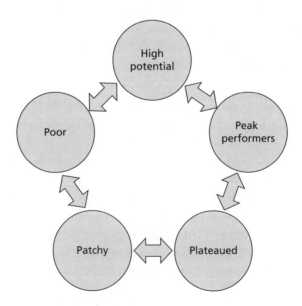

THE FIVE Ps	DESCRIPTION
High potential	These are individuals who are learning and developing in the role. They are your rising stars. They may lack some of the skills, competence or confidence for the role, but are enthusiastic and keen to learn.
Peak performers	These may be some of your best-performing team members who demonstrate their capability and confidence, and consistently deliver great results. Make sure they feel appreciated! However, beware: you may need to think about how to keep them motivated and bring in new challenges to help them grow.
Plateaued	These are people who are familiar with the job but have literally plateaued out and may be bored with what they are doing, or lack the confidence to take on new responsibilities.
Patchy	Patchy performers will have variable performance. They may be performing well in some areas and not others, or their performance will vary from day to day.
Poor	These are people who are just not performing well on a consistent basis. Their performance is below standard and needs attention.

In thinking about your team members, remember that performance may vary over time and within different aspects of an individual's role. They may have strengths in some areas of their role but not others. In addition, new responsibilities will often have a learning curve attached to them.

Team members may also move from being high potentials to performers and then plateau out, so it's important to keep the team's development at the front of your mind.

Also make sure you deal with poor performance as soon as it occurs. Many managers shy away from this and in doing so it can not only make it more difficult to deal with but also have a negative effect on the team.

What is getting in the way of good performance?

Generally, people want to do a good job and aim to gain satisfaction from their work, so it's worth thinking about the possible issues that are getting in the way of performance.

Below we have identified three gaps, 'The three Cs', which can influence an individual's performance, and impact on their ability to develop to their full potential. These are Competence, Confidence and Commitment.

COMPETENCE

Is there are gap in the skills and competence required for the role?

Do you have the resources to provide the development, coaching and supervision to help the individual develop that competence?

CONFIDENCE

Confidence can be a huge gap for some people. They may have the skills and ability but a lack of confidence or experience, or have a fear of failure which can really hold them back.

Is confidence an issue for any of your team?

COMMITMENT

Commitment and motivation can be huge issues in delivering performance and taking on new skills and responsibilities.

How motivated do think the different people in your team are?

Are you aware of what motivates them? Have you noticed any change in their motivation?

(For more on commitment and engagement revisit Chapter 11.)

Figure 14.2 The three Cs of performance

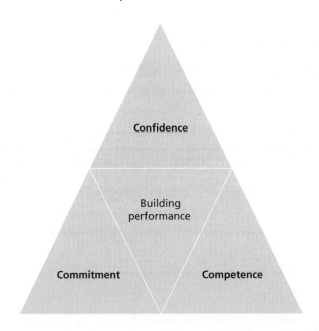

PERSONAL CIRCUMSTANCES

One other area which has a huge impact on performance is the individual's personal circumstances. Health issues, personal and family challenges all have an impact on performance and will need to be taken into account.

Here are some suggestions for managing poor performance:

- Discuss the issue and provide clear feedback, explaining the consequences of continued poor performance.
- Try to understand the root cause of the issue.
- Explore all the options and alternatives available to help bring the person back on track.
- Agree next steps and clear objectives for improvements.
- Establish regular review meetings to monitor progress.
- Provide training and coaching if appropriate.
- Monitor and document progress.

Recognising strengths

As well as recognising the gaps and development needs of your team members it is also important to recognise their strengths:

- What do they do best?
- When do you see them most motivated and enthusiastic?

When people are doing things they are good at, they generally enjoy them and want to do more. If you can tap into your team's strengths you will be tapping into what motivates them. In addition, if people are working with their strengths they will feel more confident, and more inclined to tackle some of the more challenging parts of their role.

FINDING THE RIGHT DEVELOPMENT OPPORTUNITIES

A recent CRF report[2] refers to the importance of the 70:20:10 ratio for development. This describes the fact that 70% of development should be on the job, 20% through others and 10% through formal training, illustrating just how important your role as a team leader and coach is. It also means that you need to think creatively about how to develop your team members, rather than just relying on formal training programmes.

You probably have more tools in your 'on-the-job development toolbox' than you realise. Look at the ideas below and identify how many you use. If you are lucky enough to get plenty of support from your organisation, that's great. If not, you can use these tools creatively to build a development framework with and for your team.

Remember, you don't need to be responsible for all the development activities. Your role is to facilitate the individual's development and help to set up the relevant opportunities. Other team members or people outside the team who have the specific skill or competence are often the best to take on the development role.

YOUR DEVELOPMENT TOOLKIT

Below we have described 10 development tools which are explained in more details with ideas to put them into practice:

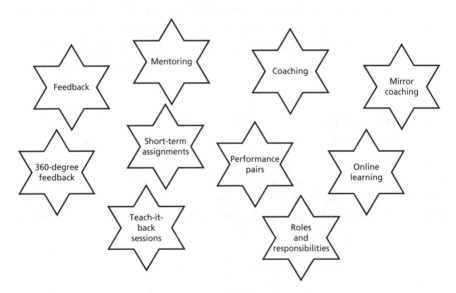

Feedback
Feedback is probably the most useful development tool. Regular and specific feedback can help to keep people on track and build their confidence. It is also valuable to obtain feedback from other people to gain a full picture of the person's performance.

Mentoring

Having a mentor can be invaluable. A mentor is someone who is usually more experienced. They can be from outside the team, and their role is to provide ideas and advice to help the individual progress. Mentoring is often useful for new hires, to help them 'learn the ropes'. It is also valuable for high flyers, to help them navigate the structure, culture and politics of the organisation. Some organisations have also introduced 'upward' mentoring where younger, media-savvy members of staff can mentor senior managers.

Coaching/co-coaching

Coaching people on an individual basis can provide specific targeted development, with the advantage of focusing directly on a work-based issue. You may be the best person to conduct the coaching, or you may want to think about using the more experienced members of your team to take on this role.

Mirror coaching

Often referred to as shadowing, this is a way of developing a new skill or competence by working alongside someone who is more experienced. It can be targeted to a specific competence. For example, if one of your team needs to understand how to chair project meetings, let them spend time with someone who is more experienced and does this well. If the shadowing is combined with coaching and feedback it can help the person to practise and develop their own approach.

360-degree feedback

360-degree feedback is a formal feedback process, where the feedback from different sources is generally anonymous. Gaining feedback from your boss, your colleagues, direct reports and even customers, can provide a valuable insight into the strengths and development areas of an individual. There are different forms of 360-degree feedback. In its simplest form you can just ask a couple of questions:

- What does this individual do well in their role?
- What could they do to improve their performance?

To keep the anonymity it is often good if someone else can collate the feedback.

More sophisticated 360-degree tools are completed online and can be designed around specific competences and behaviours.

360-degree is a particularly useful tool for more experienced team members, and people who are managing a team or working with a range of different people.

Short-term assignments

A great way of understanding more about your role and developing new ideas is to take a short-term assignment in a different department or even at a customer's site. One global organisation we work with makes a point of providing high-potential staff with the opportunity to work overseas to gain greater understanding of different cultures and business operations. They often bring back new insights and ideas to their home team, and in addition gain a greater appreciation of the global context of the organisation. If you don't have time for a short-term assignment you could think about visiting other organisations or departments.

Roles and responsibilities

When you think about how to allocate the different responsibilities, tasks and projects to team members it is worth thinking about how you can use this to develop the team and help them acquire new skills. You may also want to look at your own role and think about areas you could delegate which would help others to grow. One way of building greater flexibility into your team is to build in understudy roles so that people can learn about different areas and are more able to support and cover for each other. This can also be helpful for providing holiday and sickness cover.

Insight

One manager talked about how she tries to develop her team:

They are a bright team and keen to develop so I have devised a number of projects, which will both help them develop their strengths and help the department as well. One person who is good with spreadsheets is collating the monthly management information we need. Another is working on developing and understanding our stakeholders so we can work more effectively with them.

TAKE AWAY

Help people to develop their strengths by allocating tasks which will stretch them.

Performance pairs

Putting people together to work on a specific area or project can be really helpful. Matching more experienced team members with newer people can work well. The more experienced team member is given the role as coach so that they can help the other person get up to speed. You can also put people together who have a different blend of skills so that they can learn from and complement each other.

Online resources

The growth of online learning and e-learning virtual resources can be a real help in developing your team. From more formal program such as Coursera to management information provided by sites such as Virtual Ashridge, Mind Tools and TED talks, there is a wealth of readily accessible information available for all levels.

Try this

Pick a topic that you and your team are interested in, such as time management or team building, and ask them to research and come up with some ideas and tools the team could use. Alternatively, you can use this for individual development initiatives relating to a specific competence, such as presentation skills, which one team member may need to develop.

Teach-it back sessions

A fantastic way of learning about something is to present it back to others. If someone has been on a training programme, give them the challenge of presenting back any useful tools and ideas to the team. This technique is also useful if the team needs to understand a new system or process which is being introduced. It also has the added advantage of building confidence and credibility with others. Buddy up with another team to extend your options. Often a short 15–30 minute session is a great insight into a new topic.

FORMAL DEVELOPMENT PROGRAMMES

Formal development programmes are equally important and can provide valuable insights and learning which can be applied back at work. Ashridge research has shown that time spent preparing clear learning goals with a manager before the programme, and then debriefing the programme and providing support back at work can have a huge impact on the learning transfer from this type of development[3].

Formal training programmes are most useful when:

- They focus on specific development which cannot be provided in the organisation. This may be in technical skills such as IT or finance, or in more behavioural skills such as influencing and performance management.
- They prepare people for new roles in the organisation such as first line management, or leadership development for more strategic roles.
- They provide relevant development with outcomes which can be directly implemented.
- They focus on real work issues and challenges.
- The individual has the support of their manager in reviewing the learning and making any changes.
- The programme is built into the individual's overall development plan.

Developing the five Ps and working with the three Cs

Once you have identified where your team members are in terms of the five Ps and three Cs, and have reflected on the different development tools available, you are then in a position to tailor a development plan with and for each individual. Here are some development suggestions for the five Ps:

High potentials	• Identify the strengths and development areas. • Make sure you provide plenty of development opportunities ranging from specific training, feedback, mentoring and mirror coaching. • Have an incremental development plan. Make sure you target specific competences and review progress before moving on to new areas.
Peak performers	• 360-degree feedback will be a good tool to review the individual's strengths and development areas. • Develop their coaching skills so that they can support any newer, less experienced member of the team. • Look at developing new competences and helping the individual prepare for their next role. This may be through extra responsibilities, mentoring, short-term assignments or formal training.
Plateaued	• Understand more about the individual's strengths, interests and commitment. • Look at creating a plan which will help them develop their role and learn new skills. • Think about setting them up as a performance pair with another person so that they can pass on their skills.
Patchy	• Make sure you provide feedback on the areas where the individual is performing well and where they could improve. • It is important to find out the reason for the patchy performance. Is it competence, confidence or commitment? • Think together about how to build on the strengths and develop the weaker areas. • Set some specific objectives and take time to regularly review progress.

▶

Poor	• Make sure you tackle the poor performance and be clear about the consequences of not improving.
	• Try to understand why their performance has dropped.
	• Work together to set up an improvement plan with regular progress reviews.
	• Often techniques such as performance pair and mirror coaching can help to bring the individual up to standard.

Setting up the development plan

In working with team members to put together a development plan, you also need to think about:

- the individual's strengths, development needs and aspirations
- the challenges the team is facing now and in the future
- the skills and competences your overall team needs to survive and thrive.

Discuss these challenges with the team as some of them may like to take on new challenges and contribute ideas to help build the overall capability of the team.

Use the following table to help create a personal development plan:

Development Plan Name: Date: Review date:	
Objective What do you want to achieve?	
Outcome How will you measure your success?	
Support What support do you need?	
Development initiative What will you do to achieve your goal?	
Progress review How are you progressing?	

7 ideas for successful development planning

1 Individual development must be aligned with business goals and priorities.

2 Make sure you develop the plan with the individual, as it's important that you have their buy-in and commitment.

3 It is often a good idea to ask team members to self-assess and think about their own strengths and development needs before the meeting.

4 Remember to build in development objectives which focus on building their strengths as well as developing weaker areas.

5 Build in time to review progress on a quarterly basis and set new development goals.

6 It is important to set aside time for reflection, in order to consolidate and embed the learning.

7 Reflect on people's personality and style. We all learn in different ways so different approaches will work for different team members.

Top tips

- Identify and deal with any performance issues immediately and try to understand what is causing the issue and how to rectify it.

- Recognise the strengths of different team members and encourage them to develop and use these in the role.

- Identify development opportunities for each of the team.

- Encourage team members to support each other's development through co-coaching and sharing their expertise.

- Ensure all team members have a clear development plan.

Summary

As well as thinking about your team's development it is also important to reflect on your own development.

- How can you build on your strengths and develop your potential?

- What development needs do you have to work effectively in your current role?

- How do you need to develop yourself for future roles?

If your team sees that you are focusing on your own development they are more likely to understand how important it is to continually grow.

Actions from this chapter

ACTION	TIME FRAME	TEAM INVOLVEMENT	REFLECTIONS AND PROGRESS REVIEW
1.			
2.			
3.			

Review: Focus on people

The Focus on people section has provided an overview of four of the game-changing elements which will influence your team. Building engagement and motivation is the first element, and this requires an understanding both of what motivates the individuals in the team and what will help them to buy into the overall goal of the team and the organisation. We then looked at how to help your team to build their levels of personal and team resilience, so that you are able to manage the challenges and changes that may come your way. Linked to this was the importance of building trust, as trust is the glue which will bind the team together. Finally, we looked at how you can develop the potential of your team, working together to build your strengths and skills.

Figure 14.4 Focus on people

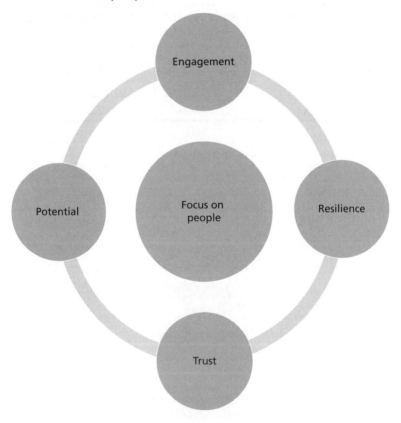

Personal skills assessment: Focus on people

Complete the assessment below to reflect on what you have taken away and applied from this section of the book.

Use a scale of 1–5 where:

1 = Never

2 = Rarely

3 = Sometimes

4 = Often

5 = Always

Circle your answer.

	YOUR ASSESSMENT 1 2 3 4 5
I am aware of what motivates each member of the team.	1 2 3 4 5
The team members are engaged and committed to the overall team goal.	1 2 3 4 5
As a team we discuss any stress points and support each other through difficult times.	1 2 3 4 5
I try to provide a positive work environment and encourage people to speak to me if they are feeling under stress.	1 2 3 4 5
I try to create a good balance between trust and accountability in the team.	1 2 3 4 5
There is a high degree of respect and cooperation amongst team members.	1 2 3 4 5
All team members have a personal development plan.	1 2 3 4 5
I am aware of the capabilities we need to develop in the team to meet the challenges we face now and in the future.	1 2 3 4 5

Personal reflection: Focus on people

What have been the most important messages, skills or ideas that you have taken away from this section?

How have you been able to apply this learning with your team and what results have you seen?

LEARNING	HOW HAVE YOU APPLIED THIS?	WHAT WAS THE RESULT?

Are there any aspects from the 'Focus on people' section that you need to refer back to for your own development?

You may want to refer back to the relevant chapters and work though some of the activities and questionnaires with your team.

Focus on communication

Along with focusing on outcomes and people, a team coach needs to focus on communication. Whether you and your team meet every day in the office or are spread out globally, communication is the glue that will pull you all closer together

Chapter 15 will focus on four game-changing aspects of team communication. It will start with the conversations you have with team members, and with the team as a whole, exploring how you can manage conflict and help your team to develop greater levels of trust and collaboration.

An important element of any team communication is the meetings you hold. Research indicates that half the meetings people attend are seen as a waste of time, and 31 hours per month are spent in unproductive meetings, so it is well worth reviewing your approach. Chapter 16 will help you develop some new and effective ways to run meetings which the team will value and look forward to.

We all work in a different team environment and context. Increasingly, people are working virtually, and across cultures. Understanding how to communicate effectively from a distance is something that many managers struggle with. Virtual teams are different from face-to-face teams, and Chapter 17 will help you to understand how to adapt and develop your approach to work effectively from a distance.

Finally, the last chapter in this section, Chapter 18, will help you to focus on your team and design a communications plan which is tailored to the team and the outcomes you need to achieve together.

Figure 14.5 Four game-changing aspects of team communication

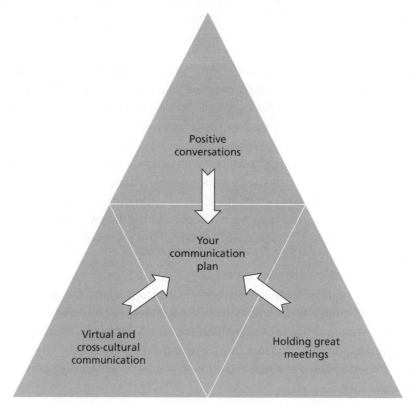

Positive conversations

Turning difficult conversations into positive ones is a challenge. Many managers feel poorly equipped to deal with these situations and are often afraid of the consequences.

Yet the cost of not having such conversations is a heavy one. It can affect productivity, customer satisfaction and team morale. Like the grains of sand falling through an hourglass, the problem or issue can build into something much bigger and more difficult to solve.

Equally difficult is the issue of team conflict, as ignoring this can mean that team members will become disengaged and even opt out altogether.

In this chapter we will look at:

- the power of positive conversations in helping to build relationships and grow performance
- the skills and strategies to enable you and the team to have positive conversations
- the ability to recognise and leverage team conflict to help the team to achieve its potential.

Positive conversations and how to have them

A good conversation is a positive exchange of ideas or information between two or more people *which leads to a workable outcome.*

Positive conversations can be a powerful force for change in the team. They can reduce misunderstandings, uncover deeper issues which might be hindering team performance, build relationships and bring new approaches and ideas into the team.

The sheer act of referring to a conversation as difficult will create fear and engender negativity, so instead, try to see all conversations as a chance to move things on and build a positive outcome for everyone.

PREPARING FOR A POSITIVE CONVERSATION

Preparation is one of the most important aspects for turning a difficult conversation into a productive one. By really considering the issues, and planning your approach and behaviour, you will have a greater chance of achieving a positive outcome.

There are three aspects to any conversation:

1 the issue
2 the context in which you are working
3 the relationship between the individuals.

All three need to be taken into account when talking to your team members.

Figure 15.1 Positive conversations

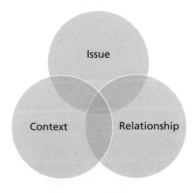

The issue

The first task is to identify the real issue and understand any underlying concerns which may be influencing the situation.

Insight

As one team leader said:

One of my team members wasn't delivering his reports on time. When we spoke about it he complained that he wasn't receiving the correct information from colleagues based in a different site. When I followed this up it became obvious that the colleagues were under pressure and hadn't been adequately trained to deal with these requests. We were able to rectify the situation and rebuild the relationship which was getting quite strained.

TAKE AWAY

Try to uncover the real issue, there is usually an underlying reason for any problem.

The context

We also need to consider the context surrounding the issue. For example, in virtual teams issues can get amplified by distance. Cultural 'norms' and language differences can create challenges. On top of this, constant change, the pressure of work and different expectations can fuel discontent.

The relationship

The third element is the relationship you have with the other person. It's always important to reflect on what is going on for them. What issues might they be facing? What else might be contributing to the issue? In addition you need to focus on your own behaviour and personality. What is your usual style and how can you adapt? We often think that we should treat people as we like to be treated ourselves. However, in reality, as one manager pointed out: 'It's not what you say; it's how it lands with the other person.'

Use the positive conversations checklist on the next page to help you prepare and reflect on your approach.

Issue	What is the issue?
	How important is it to tackle it?
	What outcome would you like to achieve?
	What assumptions are you and others making?
	Is this realistic? If not what might be a more workable outcome?
	What impact will this have on you, the team and the individual?
Context	Think about the context you are working in:
	● How is this affecting the situation?
	● What impact is this having?
	● How can you plan the conversation to take this into account?
Relationship	Put yourself in the other person's shoes:
	● What is going on for them?
	● What pressures are they under?
	● What is their style and approach?
	● How do you need to adapt your approach?

Honing your skills: the eight-step approach

In Chapter 2 we focused on the skills of being an effective team coach and looked at the SOFA feedback model. It is well worth refreshing your knowledge and revisiting that chapter.

In addition, the eight-step approach to positive conversations described below acts as a useful framework for any positive conversation.

Figure 15.2 The eight-step approach for a positive conversation

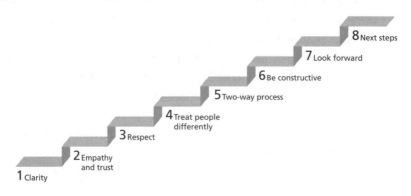

- **Step 1: Clarify the situation** It's important to clarify the situation. Always listen and focus on what the other person has to say. Ask questions to develop your ability to see the situation from the other person's perspective.

- **Step 2: Demonstrate empathy and trust** Displaying empathy and understanding will build trust and help the conversation to move ahead in a positive manner.

- **Step 3: Show respect** Showing respect for others is essential. This will come through listening and showing empathy. If you are feeling negative about the person, it will leak out in your body language and attitude and affect the conversation.

- **Step 4: Treat people differently** Remember to treat people differently. Adapt your approach to match theirs, thinking about whether they have a head, heart or gut preference.

- **Step 5: Make it a two-way process** Any good conversation is a dialogue, not a monologue, so make sure there is a good balance in the conversation. Ask questions and encourage the other person to talk.

- **Step 6: Be constructive** Build on the positives, provide good feedback and look for practical ideas and options to improve the situation.

- **Step 7: Look forward** Rather than focusing on the past and what went wrong, look into the future, and focus on how to improve the situation.

- **Step 8: Agree next steps** Agree the next steps and actions. It's a good idea to get the other person to summarise what they will do as this will demonstrate their understanding and commitment.

Coaching suggestions for difficult situations

Here are three suggestions from the world of professional coaching which will help you to keep the conversation on track.

Manage your emotions

Try to keep your emotions in check, and recognise how you are feeling. If you are feeling frustrated and angry, rather than raising your voice it is better to recognise and discuss what is happening: 'I'm feeling really frustrated as we are just not moving ahead on this issue. What can we do to move forward?'

MAINTAIN POSITIVE RAPPORT WITH THE OTHER PERSON

We talked about rapport in Chapter 2 and one of the common things that happen in times of conflict is that rapport gets broken as people's body language and voice tone change. Facial expressions get set, and defensive postures such as arm folding and finger pointing become common.

One way of diffusing the conflict is to maintain positive rapport. Listen and ask questions to explore the situation in more detail. Giving the other person a chance to talk the issue through can often reduce the emotional impact, and by maintaining positive rapport you will end up having more of a discussion than an argument.

DEMONSTRATE UNCONDITIONAL POSITIVE REGARD

Carl Rogers, often referred to as the father of coaching, talks about the importance of *unconditional positive regard*[1]. This means taking a non-judgemental approach and showing empathy and respect. This approach will help you to focus on the issue, and you will both be in a better place to generate options and ideas.

PERSONAL SKILLS CHECK

This is a useful checklist to refer to before any conversation and to review your performance again after the conversation.

		YES	NO	SOMETIMES
1	I encourage others to talk.			
2	I listen carefully.			
3	I always clarify (and summarise) key points.			
4	I find it easy to see other people's point of view.			
5	I flex my style to gain rapport with the other person.			
6	I ask questions to explore and understand the issue.			
7	I am aware of my non-verbal behaviour and attentive to other people's.			
8	I prepare well for any conversation.			
9	I always treat people with respect.			
10	We agree actions and steps at the end of the conversation.			

Be honest in your self-appraisal and set yourself some goals to improve and enhance your skills.

From individuals to teams

Dealing with team interaction and conflict is an important element of overall communication. In most teams there are 'critical moments' when tempers will flare and voices are raised. With careful facilitation these critical moments can help the team to find new and better ways of working. However, if the situation is ignored the conflict can escalate, leading to disengagement, demotivation and even jeopardising the overall success of the project.

In helping and coaching the team through times of conflict it is very important to understand why it is happening, and understand both the context of the conflict and the relationships involved.

UNDERSTANDING THE CONTEXT

Team conflict can typically arise:

- when project teams have reached a midpoint where the processes and ways of working together are not meeting the overall needs of the team
- at times of intense pressure and stress
- when there is a lack of structure and unclear roles and expectations
- when goalposts are changed
- when there is pressure from other stakeholders.

Insight

One manager describes how he dealt with a team conflict situation:

In my factory there was a lot of misunderstanding about the process of developing the product and getting it to market. This was causing conflict as people were just not aware of how everything needed to work together. Once I understood the source of the conflict, I was able to work with the

▶

team to improve the situation. We had a team day where I got the team to replicate the process. Some of the team acted as the product, others as the production, finishing, sales, and packing areas. We were able to better understand the challenges each area faced and work on some ideas to improve the process.

TAKE AWAY

Take time to understand the context and the source of conflict and then work with the team to develop a way forward.

SUGGESTIONS FOR UNDERSTANDING MORE ABOUT THE CONTEXT

- Listen and enquire to find out more about what is happening.
- Take a solutions-focused approach, looking at 'What would be happening if everything was working well?', 'What needs to happen to improve the situation?' and 'What can we do to move things ahead?'
- Test out some of the assumptions people are holding – there may be assumptions about people's responsibilities, roles, quality standards and delivery times which are affecting the situation.
- If you are working in virtual and global contexts, try to build relationships with key stakeholders in the different locations so you can get an insight in the challenges others are facing.

UNDERSTANDING THE RELATIONSHIPS

Understanding more about the relationships and different personalities in the team is essential, as this will help you to understand more about how people will react and what is important to them.

On the next page is a list of some of the typical team types, their attitude to conflict and some coaching suggestions you could use.

TEAM TYPE	TYPICAL BEHAVIOUR	COACHING SUGGESTIONS
Detonator	They are good at throwing in a killer comment to raise the critical issues.	Listen and ask clarification questions. This may open up a wider team discussion.
Strong silent type	They may have strong views but do not share them. However, their frustration will leak out through their body language.	Observe carefully and invite them to share their views, or have a quiet chat at coffee break to uncover what is on their mind.
Energiser	They have a positive 'can do' attitude and feel nothing is impossible.	Build on the positive energy but make sure they don't take on too much, and ask questions to test out their thinking.
Mediator	This is someone who always tries to find a solution which will work for everyone, even if it is not possible.	Make sure you uncover what their own views are.
Deflator	This person always sees a problem with everything.	Help the individual realise that evaluation is important but that it can kill creativity.
Blamer	The problem is always someone else's fault.	Listen, check out any assumptions and ask what they could do.
Emotional blackmailer	This person can use emotions to get their own way, having angry outbursts, tears or storming out of the room.	Discuss the situation on a one-to-one basis, and help them develop more positive ways to express themselves.
Ghost member	This person lacks the confidence to contribute ideas. They may try and offer their ideas to you outside the meeting.	Praise their ideas offline when they bring them up and encourage them to speak up in meetings knowing they have your support.

Reflect on your team meetings and look at the patterns of behaviour. Your team will have a whole mix of personalities and behavioural patterns. Think about the positive patterns of behaviour.

- What happens when the team is working well?
- How do you recognise when the team is struggling or moving into conflict?

As a team coach, knowing when and how to intervene is extremely important.

- Listen to the discussion carefully. Who is talking? Who is being quiet? What is their body language telling you?
- Notice your own reactions and feelings.
- If you notice signs that the team is struggling or moving into conflict, it's important to intervene.
- Do this by summarising where the discussion is going, and describe what you are noticing.
- At this stage it may be good to have a break to let emotions settle and give people time for reflection.
- When people return, think about a suitable question to pose to the group such as 'How can we reach our goal with minimum conflict?' or 'What do we need to do to work more effectively together?'
- You can either address this as a whole team or split into trios and pairs to discuss and share their ideas. This has the advantage of changing the dynamic, creating some energy and making sure quieter people get their views heard.
- When you have some agreement about how to move ahead, make sure you and the team follow up on any actions and review your progress at the next meeting.

Another way of tackling the concerns of the team, before it bubbles over into conflict or stress, is to find ways of generating a discussion where everyone can have a say about how they feel. Here are a few ideas you might want to consider:

- Positives and concerns – ask the team to list all their ideas about what is going well and what they are concerned about on sticky notes. Stick them up on a board, look for themes and discuss how you can build on what is going well and tackle the concerns.

- Refer back to Chapter 4 to build a better understanding of the team. You may also want to think about completing a psychometric questionnaire to explore different approaches and preferences in the team. Some questionnaires, such as the Strength Deployment Inventory[2] or the Thomas-Kilmann[3] questionnaire, are especially designed to understand more about conflict.

- Mood o gram – this is a good technique to use halfway through a project (see Figure 15.3). Ask the team to individually chart their mood over time from the beginning of the project to the present time. Combine the individual charts into a team mood o gram. Discuss the different profiles and identify how, as a team, you can ensure that everyone has a positive profile as you move into the next phase. Figure 15.3 illustrates the different experiences of three people who were working on the same project.

Figure 15.3 Mood o gram

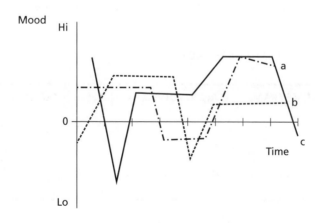

Top tips

- See all conversations as a chance to move things along.
- Prepare well and plan for any conversation you have with the team or individual team members.
- Don't underestimate the power of listening and asking good open questions.
- Maintain positive rapport and make unconditional positive regard your mantra at all times, especially in conflict.
- Recognise when the team may be facing times of conflict and challenge, and work through this with them.
- It important to recognise that healthy debate is good. It creates new ideas and shows where people's passions lie.
- Don't avoid conflict. Those tricky conversations can be some of the most useful ones you have.

Summary

Communication with the individuals, the team and between team members is a real game-changer. Improving the quality and frequency of the conversations you and your team have will go a long way to creating a more positive, open culture, which will fuel collaboration, creativity and better decision-making.

Actions from this chapter

ACTION	TIME FRAME	TEAM INVOLVEMENT	REFLECTIONS AND PROGRESS REVIEW
1.			
2.			
3.			

Holding great meetings

How many meetings do you go to that leave you energised, and feeling that it was time well spent? If you are typical of most managers your response will be 'Too few'. Does either of the scenarios below reflect your situation?

- Your email has just pinged. It's another meeting request along with an attachment containing the meeting agenda. You have been asked to block out two hours for this meeting. This is the fifth meeting invite this week and it is only Tuesday. You have an all too familiar sinking feeling in the pit of your stomach . . . you are experiencing the 'YAM' (Yet Another Meeting) factor.

- Back in January you spent time scheduling diaries for your whole team to ensure that they booked in regular team meetings throughout the year. Everyone committed to the dates, but each month when the meeting comes round, you find the drop-off rate increases right at the last moment. The excuses are often genuine but this is also a cause of frustration for you.

Your challenge is to reverse this process and work with your team to make meetings meaningful, valuable and worth the time and effort of attending. When it is estimated that 15% of an organisation's collective time is spent on meetings[1], re-thinking your approach could deliver real bottom-line results.

The purpose of this chapter is to:

- review your current approach to the meetings you currently host and attend
- develop some new approaches and ideas which will add spice and have people coming back for more
- involve your team in delivering great meetings – it's everyone's responsibility.

Where does it all go wrong?

There are many reasons why meetings are not delivering the results they should. Look at the list below and assess which reasons apply to the meetings you attend or are responsible for:

- Not relevant to you – have you ever sat through a two-hour meeting where just one item was important to you?
- Too long – our concentration spans are limited and with the added pressure of the 'day job', long meetings can just be a waste of time.
- Badly managed and facilitated – this leads to time wasting, people hijacking the meeting, and general chaos.
- Too many people – as numbers increase, you need to think about the design and format of the event to make sure everyone can be involved.
- Lack of preparation – no agenda or papers before the meeting, and no time to prepare and read them.
- No involvement – a one-way discussion, with 100 PowerPoint slides in a darkened room is one way to kill a meeting.
- No agreement, actions or follow-up.
- Multi-tasking in the meeting – people can't concentrate on two things at once and multi-tasking affects the whole team dynamic.
- Non-attendance – when people drop out at the last minute or arrive late it dilutes the effectiveness of any decisions.

Hopefully, by the end of the chapter you will have identified ways to tackle some, if not all of these issues.

What's in it for them? (WIFT)

You won't get people attending and being engaged in a meeting if there is nothing in it for them. Research by Atlassian[2] identified that when people attend meetings they rarely have a positive experience. Figure 16.1 highlights some of the main complaints people have.

Figure 16.1 Meetings statistics

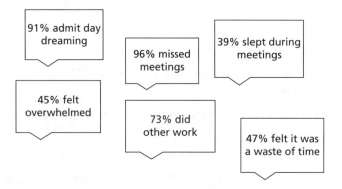

> ## Insight
> One manager we talked to had difficulty getting people to attend meetings. He realised that people were under pressure, and that while they were sitting in a meeting they felt they were losing valuable sales opportunities:
>
> *I tried to think what would work for them. They spend a lot of time on the road so I decided to start each meeting with an update, and made sure I had some interesting piece of fresh head office information which was relevant to them. They liked the idea of feeling they were the first to know what was happening and this was a real incentive to attend. I worked on being really slick, focusing on the targets and challenges important to them. I also allowed them the space to talk, and actioned many of their ideas. We*

▶

built in a pre-meeting breakfast and catch-up, which made sure everyone was there from the start. We banned technology in the meeting but had regular breaks and made sure the meeting finished with time for people to get home and catch up on the day.

TAKE AWAY

Design the meeting with the team in mind and always think about *'What's in it for them?'*

Top tips

Suggestions for constructing a team-friendly agenda:

- Make sure the agenda looks interesting – focus on outcomes and think about the WIFT factor.
- Think about travel time and time zones so that the event is feasible for everyone.
- Build in time for a team catch-up at the beginning.
- Schedule agenda items so that people who don't need to attend the whole meeting can leave after their item has been covered.
- Take time out for breaks and review how the meeting is going halfway through.

Great meetings don't just happen, they need willing participants not prisoners, and on the organiser's part, a little preparation and planning. The way to turn this around is to put yourself in the audience's shoes:

- What's important for them?
- What do they want from the meeting?
- What are their challenges and constraints?
- How can you make it worthwhile?

You may also want to think of the personalities in the team, using the Head, Heart and Gut model. The team members in the example above were very much Gut people, focused on delivery and action. What about your team? Look at the table on the following page and think about how you can adapt and develop your meetings to reflect the make-up of the team, and ensure that you design meetings which pay attention to the facts, the people issues and the outcomes.

HEAD	HEART	GUT
Create a 'thinking environment' where people come together to share ideas and debate intellectually. What latest industry reports or data are available? Provide news from the top, a chance to get more clarity on the strategic goals or internal processes. Invite stakeholders from different parts of the business to share knowledge. Make sure the agenda and any supporting information is sent out prior to the meeting. *Focus on information.*	Create a 'sharing environment' where people have the opportunity to catch up and be together. Create a social space: pay attention to the networking opportunities that coming to the meeting will provide. Pay attention to the environment: make sure the space is a pleasant one to join. Make sure you pay attention to people issues as well as the more technical/ financial issues. Make sure people are appreciated for their contribution. *Focus on people.*	Create an 'action environment' where people will get the tools to help them achieve their goals more efficiently. Sell the benefits based on outputs and how it will positively impact the team. Ensure there are quick wins. Gut people may benefit from short, snappy meetings that have clear relevance to what they are doing. Provide clarity on the purpose of the meeting and what it will help the team achieve. *Focus on action.*

One way to find out how successful your team meetings are is to get some feedback from the team.

Try this

After your next meeting ask the team to complete this review anonymously.

	PLEASE SCORE ON A FIVE-POINT SCALE: 1 MEANS STRONGLY DISAGREE AND 5 MEANS STRONGLY AGREE		
	STATEMENT	SCORE	COMMENTS
1	I felt the meeting was worth the investment of my time.		
2	I thought the meeting was the right length of time.		
3	Everybody had equal time to talk.		
4	I was able to contribute easily.		
5	There was a good team atmosphere.		
6	The right people were at the meeting.		
7	After a meeting I feel more motivated to do my job.		
8	After the meeting I feel more equipped to do my job.		
9	The outputs of the meeting were well communicated.		
10	The meeting was well facilitated.		
11	The meeting venue works well for us.		
12	The purpose of the meeting was clear.		

TIME MANAGEMENT Q1–3	DYNAMICS AND BEHAVIOUR Q4–6	OUTPUTS Q7–9	FACILITATION Q10–12
Score	Score	Score	Score

Analyse the results with the team.

- What is working well?
- What do we need to do differently?
- What should we keep on doing because it works?

- What should we stop doing?
- What could we start doing?
- When are we going to do it?
- What score do we hope for the next time we complete the questionnaire?
- How will we achieve it?

Repeat this exercise periodically, so that you can regularly review the way you are working.

Taking a little time at the end of every meeting to review how it has gone is always a good idea as it will enable you and the team to continually adapt and improve.

Involve the team

Your team are equally responsible for the success of the meeting, so build in joint responsibility by:

- involving team members in designing the event
- asking different people to be responsible for presenting different parts of the agenda (this builds in variety and makes sure people are prepared)
- electing a time keeper
- sharing the minute-taking amongst the team.

Let the team know that they are jointly responsible for the success of the meeting, so if something isn't working they need to speak up and suggest another approach.

Here are some recommendations for great face-to-face and virtual team meetings. If you are working at a distance there are more ideas in Chapter 17.

Top tips

7 recommendations for successful face-to-face meetings:

1   Start and finish on time even if you haven't covered everything.

2   Have a clear purpose and state this at the beginning.

3   Stay on track – don't allow people to railroad the meeting.

4   Involve everyone – make sure the quieter members have a chance to speak.

5   Follow up on actions and send out minutes straight after the meeting.

6   Don't allow multi-tasking . . . DEVICES OFF!

7   Whoever called the meeting should own it.

7 recommendations for successful virtual meetings:

1   Make the most of technology. Conference calls are good for catch-ups and discussion, but webinars give you more flexibility to work in real time on material and build involvement in the team.

2   Make sure people have a clear reason to attend.

3   Create clear meeting protocol. For example *calling in on time* means different things in different cultures so you need to be more specific in a virtual space.

4   Set up buffer time for people to call in early to chat, or just mute their line so you don't need to wait for others.

5   As the meeting chair, keep a careful note of who is contributing and make sure you bring in the quieter members.

6   If you are asking a question, direct it to a specific person and address them by their name, for example, 'Karin. What are your views on x?'

7   Keep the team involved by inviting them to present parts of the meeting.

In setting up a meeting you also need to think about how to create a space where people can work effectively together. Here are some recommendations. You may want to refer back to the text on facilitation in Chapter 3 if you want to look at this area again in more depth.

Top tips

7 recommendations for managing group dynamics:

1 Think about the venue and room layout. Consider removing tables and having chairs in a circle to create more discussion.

2 Don't allow your Detonators, Dominators, and Deflators, described in Chapter 15, to take the meeting off-topic.

3 Think about the audience. If you have a larger number of attendees, build in some group work and time for people to present back.

4 Mix people up so that cliques don't form and people get to hear different perspectives.

5 Always have a supply of flipcharts, pens and sticky notes which you can use to generate ideas.

6 Manage the energy in the group with breaks, fresh air and different approaches, speakers and activities.

7 Be alert to possible conflict and deal with it appropriately.

Adding spice

Keeping up the engagement and building involvement will mean that people will look forward to the meeting. The chances are that they will contribute more and feel committed to take ideas forward. Here are a few ideas on how to add spice to your meetings.

EXTERNAL SPEAKERS

Invite external speakers. These can be people from other departments in the organisation, clients, or people from different industries who stimulate creativity. For example, a chef in a busy restaurant may be able to share insights into how to develop team work, work under pressure and logistics management. A housing association invited some of their clients, and the agencies they work with, to a meeting, so that head office staff could be really connected to the people they are supporting.

GO TO A DIFFERENT LOCATION

Getting out of the office helps to remove some of the daily pressure. Think about the venue and be creative. One manager organised a meeting in the local library and 30 minutes of the day was spent listening to 'story time' with a group of young children. The reflections on this were used to think about how to get attention, what it is like to be present and focused and what stories they could use to engage their customers.

YES AND

So often ideas are killed by people putting up objections and saying 'Yes, but . . .'.

Create a rule where people say 'Yes, AND . . .', so that they can build on and develop the idea, rather than shutting it down.

TAKE A WALK AND TALK

When focusing on a problem, split the group into pairs or trios and get them to go for a walk outside to have a discussion and come back with ideas. Be clear about the time frame so everyone gets back at the right time. This is a real energiser and, interestingly, people think differently and more reflectively if they are walking.

HAVE A POP-UP MEETING

At Google there is a golden rule: 'Decisions should never wait for meetings. If a meeting needs to happen for something to get done, hold the meeting as soon as possible.'

HAVE A STAND-UP MEETING

If you want to shorten your meetings, have them standing up. Research comparing sit-down and stand-up meetings found that sit-down meetings were 34% longer and produced no better decisions than ones held standing[3].

HAVE A HANGOUT MEETING

Just getting together informally can help the team to gel. One team we know has regular 'Bun Friday' where everyone downs tools for half an hour to have a coffee and catch up. Virtual teams can benefit from virtual coffee times. It's amazing how much work also gets done when people are just catching up.

HOLD A 'WORLD CAFÉ' MEETING

The world café is a great process if you have a large group of people coming together and you want to generate ideas, encourage conversation and build connections. It involves improvising a café with tables. People sitting at the table will work on an issue, share and document ideas and then move to a different table and different group to continue the process. There is plenty of information on the web about how to run and organise this type of meeting, so if you are interested in finding out more visit **www. theworldcafe.com.**

Top tips

- Spend time thinking about getting the right people to meetings and ensure the agenda will engage them.
- Pay attention to the meeting duration and frequency.
- Involve team members before, during and after the meeting in the design, delivery and implementation phases.
- Use creativity to spice up meetings, varying the location, duration and layout of the meeting space.
- Ensure actions are communicated promptly after the meeting, with clear expectations of who is responsible for what.

Summary

As a key element of your communication strategy, having great meetings should be a number one priority. Meetings can help to create a culture of engagement. They can build performance and ensure that decisions are made swiftly, with the input of others. Use the ideas from this chapter to review your approach to meetings and work with the team to make sure that this vital communication tool can act as game-changer for the team.

Actions from this chapter

ACTION	TIME FRAME	TEAM INVOLVEMENT	REFLECTIONS AND PROGRESS REVIEW
1.			
2.			
3.			

Virtual and cross-cultural teams

Managing any team can be challenging, but managing a virtual team is on a different and sometimes more difficult dimension. A virtual team is one where team members are spread geographically and this may be across time, space and organisational boundaries. There are different degrees of virtual teaming, from the global team that never meets, to teams who are located on different floors in an office building. Even small amounts of dispersed working can affect team work and collaboration[1].

Virtual working is very much a part of our lives with 87% of respondents to a recent virtual team survey[2] indicating that 25% of their productivity depended on virtual working.

THE BENEFITS OF VIRTUAL WORKING	THE DISADVANTAGES OF VIRTUAL WORKING
Cost savings on travel Access to diverse skills Knowledge-sharing Ability to work globally Improved collaboration Faster response opportunities	Lack of identity with the team Lack of trust Cultural clashes and greater potential for misunderstandings Lack of face-to-face time Feelings of isolation Difficult to build energy and engagement

The benefits of virtual working are easy to see but gaining advantages from virtual working is very difficult. MIT found that only 18% of the 70 global business teams in their study were highly successful, and many of the reasons cited for their failure focused on the quality of communication[3]. If you can get this right it could be a real game-changer for your team.

This chapter will help you to:

- understand the challenges in virtual team and cross-cultural communication
- develop the skills and approach to lead and coach your team from a distance and across cultural boundaries
- create a framework for effective virtual team work.

The communication challenges of virtual working

Perhaps the biggest challenge in the world of virtual working is that managers and their organisations don't recognise that it is different from traditional team work, where people are co–located and have the opportunity to communicate face-to-face on a daily basis. You lose many of those informal communication and social cues, such as taking a lunch, coffee or tea break together and having a quick corridor conversation to move things along. These are all subtle elements which have an important role in progressing the team.

Research by the Economist[4] surveyed over 400 participants and identified three major challenges of managing a virtual team:

CHALLENGES	%
Misunderstandings due to differences in culture, language and inability to read people's expressions	57
Difficulty in leading teams remotely	46
Difficulty in building camaraderie and trust	44

Source: Managing Virtual Teams: Taking a more Strategic Approach, The Economist Intelligence Unit, 2009

Given that the failure rate of virtual teams is so high, it is worth looking at some of the reasons for this:

- **Lack of clear processes.** Agreeing how the team works together is essential. Face-to-face teams can be more fluid, but for a virtual team, establishing roles, responsibilities, deliverables and ways of communicating are essential. If people don't have a clear framework they won't know what to do.

- **Team relationships.** When people don't know each other and are separated by distance, it is hard for them to build trust and understanding. Reciprocity and cooperation is often based on the quality of the relationship, and if people don't build that connection they will be less likely to share knowledge and ideas.

- **Failure to capture knowledge.** Capturing and passing on knowledge can be a real challenge if you don't know how to access it and don't understand who needs it: things can fall through the net.

- **Nothing holding the team together.** Many virtual teams are pulled together for a specific purpose. They may have different reporting lines and other responsibilities, so if you are not careful the team will be pulled in different directions.

- **Lack of engagement.** If teams don't have a clear purpose, it is easy for members to become disengaged. When working virtually, this isn't as easy to notice. It's important to look for signs, such as lack of attendance at meetings, which may indicate an engagement problem.

- **Language and culture.** Working in a global team brings with it the additional complexity of language and cultural differences, which can lead to misunderstandings.

Differences between successful and unsuccessful virtual teams

When looking at successful and unsuccessful teams there are some interesting differences around the quality and quantity of communication. Successful teams spend more time on getting to know each other and having non-business conversations. They actively keep in touch and collaborate freely[5].

In addition they also have a clear focus on the task, understand their roles and responsibilities and have good communication processes in place. It is this focus on the task, the relationships and the processes which holds the team together.

Figure 17.1 Task, relationships and team performance

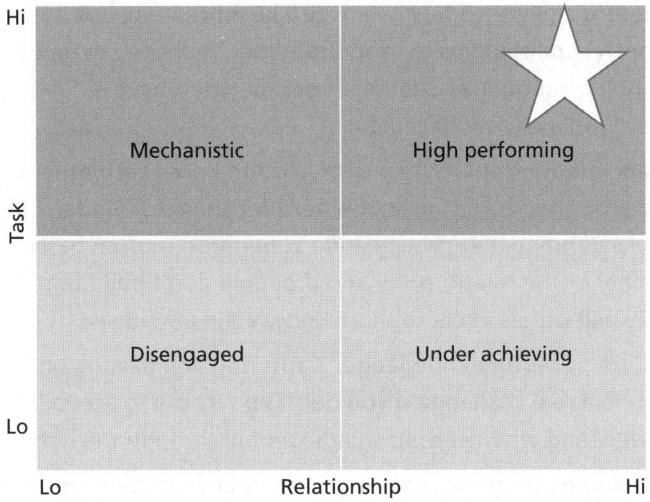

How does your team shape up?

Team working is at the heart of managing the virtual communication process and it is important to get the input and feedback from the team.

Ask team members to fill in the questionnaire on the next page.

PLEASE SCORE ON A FIVE-POINT SCALE: 1 MEANS STRONGLY DISAGREE AND 5 MEANS STRONGLY AGREE		
Our team	YOUR SCORE	COMMENTS
have a clear understanding of the team's purpose.		
are aware of the outputs and deliverables.		
have clear communication and knowledge management processes.		
understand each other's roles and responsibilities.		
actively keep in touch with each other to build relationships and trust.		
understand and manage the different cultures and language abilities in the team.		

If your team has scored:

28–30

The team is working well together and you have the right balance with an equal attention to the task, the processes and the relationships in the team.

Make sure you regularly review progress and identify how to keep improving and developing the team.

22–27

There is room for improvement in how the team works together. Look at similarities and differences between individual scores, as often in virtual teams, members will have different perceptions about how the team is working.

7–21

You really need to focus on developing the team and exploring how you can work more effectively together. Review the scores with the team and identify what you all need to do to develop your overall effectiveness.

Also look for trends:

- Statements 1 and 2 focus on the task and what the team needs to deliver.
- Statements 3 and 4 focus on the processes or how the team is working.
- Statements 5 and 6 focus on the relationships in the team.

All these aspects are important for team success.

Developing successful ways of working

Here are eight different ideas to improve team effectiveness (see Figure 17.2).

Figure 17.2 Developing successful ways of working

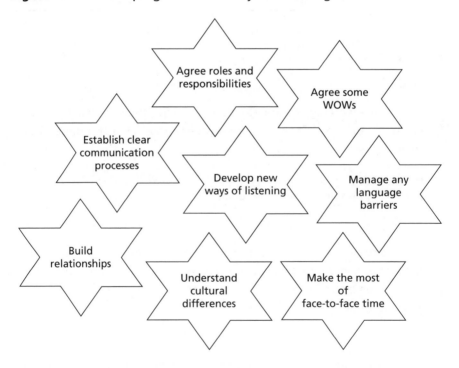

ESTABLISH CLEAR COMMUNICATION PROCESSES

Setting up a clear communication plan is essential. Schedule meetings, one-to-ones, and information management systems and find ways to encourage communication across the team.

Research by Siemens in 2012[6] found that more than four in 10 virtual team members always or frequently felt frustrated or overwhelmed by the complexity of disconnected communication technologies, so try to make sure the team is not overwhelmed, and create some systems and processes to share knowledge effectively.

AGREE ROLES AND RESPONSIBILITIES

Have clearly defined roles and responsibilities both for yourself and the team. The team needs to know what they are accountable for, how much time they have to contribute, and how the work they do relates to others. Think of your virtual team members as pieces in a jigsaw. You should all be able to see the whole picture.

Insight

As one team manager told us:

We always spend a lot of time talking about how the team works, our goals and procedures and setting high expectations for sharing information across the team. That early phase is a key time to talk to people about 'how we work around here' and what is valued. I never make the assumption that simply because someone new is experienced, they will just 'fit into' our team culture; I want to make sure that they really understand how we work.

TAKE AWAY

Make sure everyone has a clear picture of how the team fits together.

AGREE SOME WOWS

Agree clear 'Ways of Working'. This refers to the protocol and rules around meetings and emails and knowledge-sharing. It could also include agreement around working hours (especially if the team is working across time zones) and ways of communicating. (For more on this refer back to the Team Charter in Chapter 6.)

BUILD RELATIONSHIPS

There is a certain irony in the fact that those working in virtual teams are sometimes known as 'remote workers' and this can often summarise how they feel – remote!

Make sure that the team has the chance to get to know each other. Complete some training together, introduce new people and build in time to allow people to check in with each other. Encourage team members to build in social time with each other, and maintain regular contact with your team, just to see how they are.

Simple things like starting a meeting with a round of updates from everyone about what is happening for them, and celebrating birthdays and key events, can make a real difference in helping people to feel connected.

Insight

Based in London, but with a global team spread across Europe, Asia and Africa, one manager we worked with recognised this was going to be a tough challenge:

Due to travel restrictions I knew that it would be impossible to meet the whole team. The challenge for me was very much around how to build trust with the new team and help them to work together effectively. I decided to run a virtual team event. I set up different teams, mixing locations, and elected team captains from the regions, deliberately wanting them to take the lead. The first task the team had to complete was to build a collage of their team and include images of things that were important to them. This initial task was a real icebreaker and helped people to have some fun and get to know each other. It was really noticeable after the event that people seemed more comfortable communicating and helping each other out.

TAKE AWAY
Help people to feel connected by developing virtual team events.

DEVELOP NEW WAYS OF LISTENING

In the virtual world we don't always have the luxury of reading people's body language. This means that team members have to learn to listen much more to tone, pace and intonation. They have to remember to include people on calls and ask questions specifically to the individual. Virtual listening requires a lot of concentration and it is not something which can be done at the same time as completing emails. Always try to give people your attention, ask questions and provide encouragement to others. No one likes talking into an empty space!

UNDERSTAND CULTURAL DIFFERENCES

If you are working in a global team it's important to understand and discuss the cultural differences in the team. Different cultures have very different concepts of leadership, hierarchy and their role in a meeting. They also have different approaches to making decisions: for example, in Sweden decisions are made by consensus and discussion, whilst in China the leader will have the final say. The questionnaire below is a useful one to use with your team as it highlights some of these cultural dilemmas. It is also a useful discussion tool, providing the team with the opportunity to understand and agree on how to work together.

Try this

CULTURAL WORKING PREFERENCES TOOL

Ask the team to complete this by circling the number which most reflects their preference, and compile the scores onto one chart. Once you have the team profile you can look at any differences and discuss how you can manage them as a team.

The leader should make the final decisions after consulting with the group.				Decisions are best made in consensus with the whole team.		
3	2	1	0	1	2	3
Authority is derived from one's position.				Authority is earned through one's achievements.		
3	2	1	0	1	2	3

▶

One should only say things that are relevant and that are thought through.				Talking about things that simply come to mind can lead to new ideas and creativity.		
3	2	1	0	1	2	3
It is important to distinguish clearly between private and work life.				Private and work life are closely linked and it is not important to separate them.		
3	2	1	0	1	2	3
High performance is reached by focusing on one thing at a time.				To reach high performance it is necessary to work on several things at the same time.		
3	2	1	0	1	2	3
Feedback to others on their behaviour should be given to them immediately even if this is public.				Feedback to others on their behaviour should be expressed privately even if this is at a later time.		
3	2	1	0	1	2	3
Managing conflict should be done privately at an appropriate time.				Conflicts must be managed explicitly and directly in the moment.		
3	2	1	0	1	2	3
Feelings should be kept to yourself in the workplace.				Expressing how we feel is important for good working relationships.		
3	2	1	0	1	2	3
It is better if everyone speaks one at a time without interrupting.				Interrupting and speaking at the same time is a natural part of any discussion.		
3	2	1	0	1	2	3
Decisions must be made on facts and logical principles.				Decisions have to be grounded in intuition and feelings.		
3	2	1	0	1	2	3

Source: Based on the cross-cultural dimensions in the research models of Gert Hofstede, *Culture's Consequences,* and Fons Trompenaars, *Riding the Waves of Change*[7]

MANAGE ANY LANGUAGE BARRIERS

Levels of ability to speak the language of the meeting can also create a real communication barrier. Speaking slowly, using clear simple language, making sure people don't talk over each other and bringing quieter team members into the discussion can help. Often people who are working in their second language find it hard to follow discussions, so try to ensure that only one person talks at a time. Also try to make sure that people have access to important information before the meeting to help them prepare.

Insight

It is amazing how small issues can lead to misunderstandings. One of the people we interviewed for this book talked about how his German style of addressing people in emails clashed with the Australian values of a colleague, who saw his approach as being very impersonal. Neither spoke about this until a third person intervened to try and resolve the apparent conflict it was causing. As he pointed out:

It was resolved eventually but how was I supposed to understand the rules?

TAKE AWAY

Be aware of and understand any cultural differences in the team.

MAKE THE MOST OF FACE-TO-FACE TIME

If you have the opportunity for face-to-face meetings, build in social time and set the event up to encourage people to work in different groups to mix with each other. Use some of the time to review the way you are working together. Look at what is going well and encourage the team to think about how you can improve in the future.

I organised two global meetings. One was for 45 international managers from our audit division. The three-day event was highly successful. I organised another meeting for the global supply-chain team but this one didn't have the same level of engagement. When I reflected on the difference I realised that for the audit division, at the last minute I had organised a meal for the previous evening and got the team involved in planning the event. This really helped to bond the group. However, the biggest difference was that the audit team really wanted to get together as they often work in isolation on their projects and valued the opportunity to get together as a team.

TAKE AWAY

Plan carefully for any team event, build in some social time, and get the team involved in the organisation to tap into their energy and commitment.

Reflecting on your leadership approach

Virtual team work and virtual leadership is not right for everyone. As well as good technical skills, virtual leaders need to have the skills to work at a distance and across cultural boundaries. To be successful you will need to do the following.

SHARPEN YOUR VIRTUAL ANTENNAE

When you can't see what's happening in different locations it's important to develop your virtual antennae.

BE AWARE OF YOUR IMPACT

Every interaction matters when working virtually and misunderstandings can easily create conflict when working at a distance. This means that you need to make the most of every touch point with your team to build relationships.

Research has shown that in virtual teams the way that leaders approach communicating via email will influence the level of trust in teams[8]. They found that in high-trust teams, the leaders sent out early positive email messages and kept a strong, sustained focus on action and task results. So think about the tone of your emails as this is one of the main touch points with the team.

BE COMFORTABLE WITH AMBIGUITY

Working virtually requires a real mix of leadership approaches. On the one hand you need to be very clear about the roles, processes and ways of working together, especially in the start-up phase of the team. However, you need to be equally comfortable working with ambiguity, letting go and allowing team members to take a lead in communicating and making things happen.

Insight

As one 'virtual' team leader said:

I try to build relationships with managers in the different locations and get feedback about how things are going. I also notice if someone isn't emailing or joining meetings as this may be a sign that they are busy on another project or disengaged with the team. Finally, I always listen for what is not said. If someone calls to update me on where they are, I take the opportunity to chat about how things are going and there is usually something else that I can help with. I keep a note of who I have spoken to so I can make sure I have regular contact. I also have a photograph of the team above my desk.

TAKE AWAY

Take time to keep in touch to understand what is really happening.

Top tips

- Invest time in really getting to know one another, particularly focusing on understanding cultural difference if you are a global team.
- Have a clear understanding of the goals of the team and everyone's role within it.
- Review how you are working together and identify ways to improve.
- Develop some clear communication processes.
- Recognise that virtual teams need to develop a high degree of trust to operate well.

Summary

Team success is not a matter of whether you are a virtual or co–located team. The secret is in recognising that a virtual team is different, and as a result needs a clear and conscious focus on communicating the task, developing ways of working and building the relationships to bind the team together. This won't happen by chance. Your role is to create the right environment and coach the team to success. Think about the actions you and your team can take to improve the way you communicate and work together in the future.

Actions from this chapter

ACTION	TIME FRAME	TEAM INVOLVEMENT	REFLECTIONS AND PROGRESS REVIEW
1.			
2.			
3.			

Creating your communication plan

This chapter builds on the previous chapters in this section and will help you to develop a communication plan for the team.

You will have the opportunity to assess your current approach to communication and explore how you can work with the team to enhance the quality and effectiveness of your approach.

This chapter will ensure you are able to:

- understand and assess the effectiveness of the ways you and your team currently communicate
- identify how to improve the quality and efficiency of your communication
- create a communication strategy that is tailored to your specific context.

Before you begin

Think about the work you did in Chapter 5 around mapping the team. If you did not complete the exercises, it is well worth going back and working through them to understand more about the characteristics of your team, the type of team you are working with and some of the potential challenges you face.

In order to have a good communication strategy it is important to spend some time thinking about what you want to achieve:

- What are the goals you want to achieve?
- Who are the key people with whom you need to communicate on a regular basis?
- How do you currently communicate?
- How effective is the way you currently communicate?
- Where are the problem areas?
- What are the benefits to you and the team of having a great communication strategy?

How does the team currently communicate?

A good place to start is to reflect on the communication channels your team uses by completing and reflecting on the chart below.

Which communication channels do you use for the following team issues?

	FACE-TO-FACE	EMAIL	VIDEO CONFER-ENCING	CONFERENCE CALL	WEBINAR	OTHER
Problem-solving						
Information sharing						

▶

	FACE-TO-FACE	EMAIL	VIDEO CONFER-ENCING	CONFERENCE CALL	WEBINAR	OTHER
Feedback						
Performance reviews						
Learning						
Team building						
Networking						
Resolving interpersonal issues						
Setting objectives						

Source: Adapted from Pam Jones and Viki Holton (2006) *Teams – Succeeding in Complexity*[1]

Reflect on the balance of the different communication channels you use and whether this is the correct balance for the team.

Test out your assumptions

We all have views and preferences about the different communication channels. Many managers often feel that face-to-face meetings are the best form of communication: 'You can really build trust and eyeball each other.' However, is this true?

The reality is that often teams are more dispersed and meeting face-to-face regularly isn't an option. Our experience of virtual coaching at Ashridge demonstrates that virtual conversations can be equally valuable. As one coach pointed out: 'People often open up more over the phone. We still manage to build an effective relationship, in fact there are less distractions so we can really focus on the conversation.'

Some of the managers we talked to consciously changed the balance of communication in their team when they realised that the current approach wasn't working.

Insight

As one team leader said:

> I became annoyed with the overall reliance on email, especially when some of the team are sitting next to each other, so we had a team email ban on Fridays to encourage people to talk to each other. Interestingly, problems got solved more quickly and people are now developing new ideas together and generally having more fun.

Another team leader recognised the toll his reliance on face-to-face meetings was having on himself and others:

> I really value face-to-face meetings, and tried to meet with team members each month. However, as my team is dispersed across Europe, this was becoming too much of a burden. Communication was taking up 70% of my time! With two days a week spent out of the office, travelling to different locations, my resources were running low. I have now become much more reliant on scheduled telephone calls and webinars. The team have learned to adapt to this, and I have reduced the site visits to once every six months.

TAKE AWAY

Have the courage to change the way you communicate, and question your assumptions.

Assessing your communication effectiveness

When you are adapting the way you communicate, it is important to reflect on how the team feels about the current communication approach. It's not just the amount of communication, but also the quality and value of that communication which is important.

Use the questions below to explore the effectiveness of the current approach to communication in the team.

HOW EFFECTIVE ARE WE ON A SCALE OF 1–5 WHERE 1 IS NOT EFFECTIVE AND 5 VERY EFFECTIVE?		
	YOUR SCORE	WHAT COULD WE DO TO IMPROVE OUR APPROACH?
How well do we communicate as a team?		
How effective are we at using the different communication channels:		
• Email?		
• Face-to-face meetings?		
• Conference calls?		
• WebEx and other forms of communication?		

The more complicated your team structure, the more you will need to pay attention to how you communicate. The more dispersed your team is, the more isolated people can feel. Make sure you help to create a regular and consistent pattern to your communication, so that people feel connected with each other and with what you are trying to achieve.

Try this

Discuss your current communication process with the team. Highlight what is working and what isn't working and agree changes. Agree some communication protocol and rules for your emails and conference calls, so that you have some agreed ways of working.

Improving the way you communicate

Once you have assessed how satisfied you and the team are with the way you communicate, you may want to think about how you can improve. Here are some suggestions for making the most of emails and conference calls.

With an estimated 28% of work time spent on emails[2] it is well worth making sure that you and the team can make the most effective use of this communication channel.

Top tips

Suggestions for good email protocol

- Have a clear subject heading which describes the content.
- Make sure your content is focused; be clear about the purpose and outcome of the email.
- Keep it short. Use bullet points rather than rambling sentences.
- Proof-read before you click 'send'.
- Be polite.
- Always respond promptly and agree what the response time should be for your team.
- Just send your email to the people who need it.

▶

- Don't take your anger out on the keyboard. Put your email into the draft box and review it later when you have calmed down.

Suggestions for quality conference calls

- Like any good meeting, send out the agenda and background information prior to the meeting.
- Call in early to welcome the team.
- Start on time.
- Make sure people on the call have been introduced.
- Speak clearly and be aware of any language problems.
- Vary the times of your calls to fit in with the different time zones of the callers.
- Try to ensure that people call in from a quiet place and preferably not on a mobile.
- Use a headset.
- Limit the duration of the call.
- Make sure everyone is involved and bring in quieter members.
- Ensure that only one person speaks at a time.
- Have a moderator and note-taker.
- Set the scene well at the beginning and summarise at the end.
- Avoid distractions and don't multi-task.

Get creative about communication

The communication channels available now in many organisations provide the potential for different and equally valuable forms of communication. One team we worked with travelled frequently to different locations and the internal social networking site allowed everyone to keep in touch. As the team leader pointed out: 'For me it's a great way to stay in touch with the team and it fills many a tedious hour sitting in airport lounges.' It was also a valuable way of building relationships and connections which are the glue binding any effective team.

Insight

Another manager described the way she adapted her communication process to fit in with the preference of her younger team:

Working in a finance team, month end is a really important time. We need to work in a very efficient way, so we can pass on information and pull all the figures together. We used to rely on email but this was too cumbersome and people weren't responding in time. We then tried using mobiles but again this didn't work. One of my younger team members suggested setting up a WhatsApp group and this has completely changed the way we communicate. Everyone responds immediately and it also allows us to share regular updates . . . so much easier and more interactive than our other approaches.

TAKE AWAY

Be open to creative suggestions from within the team and try different approaches.

Sharing the responsibility for communication

One important take away from this chapter is to recognise that you can share the responsibility for communication with your team. It doesn't need to rest solely on your shoulders.

Insight

One manager described how she set up a web of communication in her team and reduced her role and responsibility as the central communication hub:

My team is a dispersed project team. I had weekly a catch-up meeting with team members, a regular team meeting and weekly email updates, and I tried to be on hand to handle any queries or problems. In addition, I was communicating with all the other stakeholders outside the team and managing upwards. I found that being the 'go to' point for everyone was

▶

putting a serious drain on my time and energy. I felt like an octopus being pulled in all directions. Instead, I decided to give more responsibility and autonomy to the team. I set up a communication network with team members having different roles and responsibilities. One looked after gathering and communicating the weekly figures, another produced the team newsletter and weekly update, another was responsible for holiday and sickness cover, and another for working with some of our stakeholder groups. We also set up some processes for sharing and storing information which meant I could access the data I needed with ease. I was able to reduce the amount of team meetings and reduce the time I spent on communication. It also had the added advantage of building interdependencies and relationships across the team and developing their skills and potential.

TAKE AWAY
Coach the team to share the responsibility for communication.

Styles and preferences: yours and theirs

Communicating and influencing go hand in hand. It is worth thinking about your own style and preferences and that of the team. Don't assume that how you like to be communicated with will be the same for others.

Consider the Head, Heart and Gut model (covered in Chapter 4).

Head people will like:

- clear logical arguments
- facts and analysis
- bullet points
- reasons and explanations.

Heart people will like:

- feedback and encouragement
- a friendly tone
- the opportunity to get to know others.

Gut people will like:

- short, to-the-point communication
- actions and deadlines
- energy and drive.

You may also want to think about whether your team members (and yourself) are more extrovert or introvert. Extroversion and introversion are two preferences in the Myers-Briggs personality questionnaire[3]. People with a preference for extroversion will get their energy from others. They will enjoy working with others, sharing ideas and are often the first to speak out in meetings. People with a preference for introversion are more reflective. They like to think things through before contributing their ideas, will prefer it when the agendas and papers for the meeting are sent out in advance, and will enjoy working alone in peace and quiet. You may want to encourage them to contribute in meetings as their more thoughtful and reflective approach will add real value to the team.

Think about your own preferences:

- How do you like to be communicated with?
- What are the preferences of your team?
- How should you adapt your approach?

Whilst you can adapt your communication for different individuals, you also need to craft an approach which meets everyone's needs, so that it provides sufficient information and detail, a call for action and demonstrates appreciation and encouragement.

Creating your plan

Who, what, when and how? These are the big questions for you when thinking about your communication plan:

- **Who** do you need to communicate with? Are there different groups and different stakeholders who you need to communicate with? Will your communication approach be the same to all these groups? Who will take responsibility for different aspects of communication in the team?

- **What** do you need to communicate? Information sharing, ideas generation, strategy updates, social activities, immediate issues, scheduling and organising, performance reviews and one-to-ones, etc.

- **When** do you need to communicate? How do you create a regular drum beat of communication? Are there particular times when it is crucial that you all get together to review progress? Do you need to make better links into the overall reporting cycles in the organisation?

- **How** do you want to communicate together? What is feasible in terms of time scales, distances and time zones? How can you get a balance with communicating information and managing the relationships in the team? How can you help to build responsibility across the team?

These questions are all important, and you can work on them with your team. Getting the balance right is essential. Too little communication and people will feel disconnected; too much and they will feel swamped with meetings and unable to focus on other aspects of their work.

Top tips

- Test the assumptions around how you are currently communicating with the team. Is it working or is there room for improvement?

- Share the responsibility for communication; you don't have to do it all yourself.

- Get creative: consider all the different mediums including social media. If you have a multigenerational team, how do people like to communicate, and what can the different generations learn from each other?

- Consider individual communication styles and preferences. Flex your style to suit the team.

- Make sure you have a clear communication strategy for your team and stakeholders.

Summary

Working on a clear communication plan with the team can be a real game-changer. So many problems in teams are a result of poor communication. Even if you are satisfied with your current communication plan, review it with the team to see if you can make any improvements. Remember that communication is not just about the contents of the communication but it is also about building relationships and developing a sense of team spirit and commitment.

Actions from this chapter

ACTION	TIME FRAME	TEAM INVOLVEMENT	REFLECTIONS AND PROGRESS REVIEW
1.			
2.			
3.			

Review: Focus on communication

'Focus on communication' has considered the importance of team communication and the challenges involved in getting the balance right in terms of the quality, quantity and frequency of any communication. You have had the opportunity to reflect on your approach to one-to-one conversations, looking at how to develop a positive approach to even the most difficult conversation, and how to manage and work with any conflict with in the team. We went on to explore how to make the most of any meetings you hold and how to adapt your approach if you are working in a virtual or cross-cultural context.

Finally, you had the opportunity to pull this together and create a communications plan tailored to your specific team environment.

Figure 18.1 Focus on communication

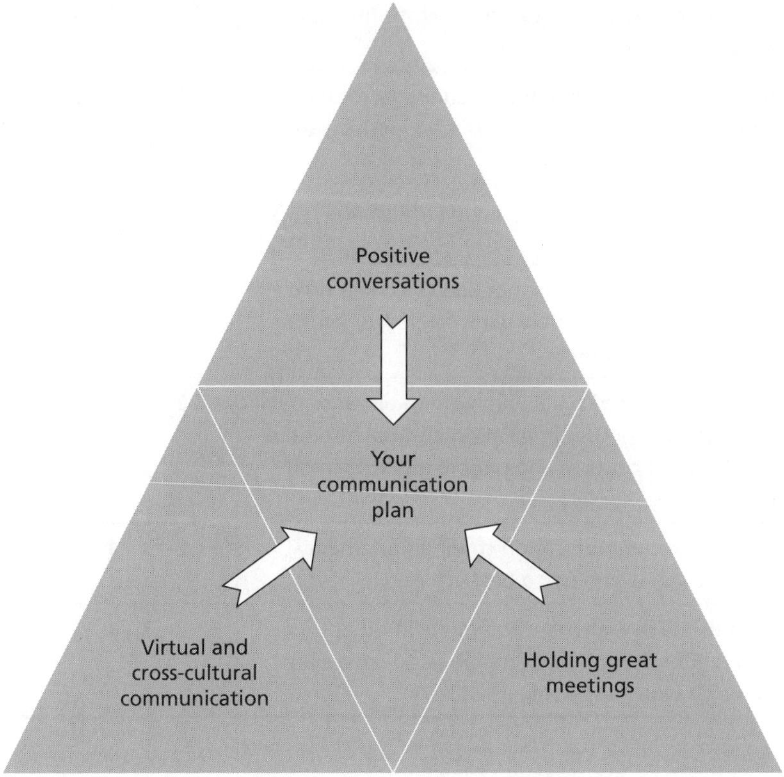

Progress review: Focus on communication

Complete the questionnaire below to reflect on what you have taken away and applied from this section of the book.

Use a scale of 1–5 where:

1 = Never

2 = Rarely

3 = Sometimes

4 = Often

5 = Always

Circle your answer

	YOUR ASSESSMENT 1 2 3 4 5
I try to make sure that all one-to-one discussions result in a positive outcome for both parties.	1 2 3 4 5
If I recognise conflict brewing in the team I try to surface the disagreement, so that we can actively work towards a solution.	1 2 3 4 5
I regularly review the quality of team meetings and seek feedback to improve them.	1 2 3 4 5
I plan and structure every team meeting to reflect who is attending, the atmosphere we want to create, and the outcome we want to achieve.	1 2 3 4 5
I am aware of the type of team I am working in and adapt the meeting and communication approach to take account of different cultures and people working in different locations.	1 2 3 4 5
We use a range of communication channels and have agreed how we can use these to best effect.	1 2 3 4 5
I have assessed the overall team communication approach and gained feedback from team members to create an approach which works for us all.	1 2 3 4 5

Personal reflection: Focus on communication

What have been the most important messages, skills or ideas that you have taken away from this section?

How have you been able to apply this learning with your team and what results have you seen?

LEARNING	HOW HAVE YOU APPLIED THIS?	WHAT WAS THE RESULT?

Are there any aspects from 'Focus on communication' that you need to refer back to for your own development?

You may want to refer back to the relevant chapters in this section, and work though some of the activities with your team.

part three

Pulling it all together: A compact guide for everyday coaching situations

We hope you have enjoyed building your team coaching skills and trying out some of the practical ideas and suggestions included in each of the chapters.

Your coaching approach needs to become part of your everyday leadership style and be incorporated into every conversation and interaction you have with your team. This is not easy when, like many managers, you are working in the moment, having to juggle and respond to a range of different demands and pressures.

This part of the book provides a compact guide and ready reference for many of the coaching situations and challenges you may face.

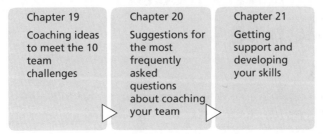

Chapter 19	Chapter 20	Chapter 21
Coaching ideas to meet the 10 team challenges	Suggestions for the most frequently asked questions about coaching your team	Getting support and developing your skills

Chapter 19 provides a range of easily actioned coaching suggestions for 10 of the common team challenges managers face. You can use this section as a pocket guide for extra inspiration and support when you are working with your team.

Chapter 20 focuses on many frequently asked questions (FAQs) faced by managers as they put their coaching skills into practice. It provides a quick reference guide and support for those tricky situations which you may be unsure about.

Finally, the concluding chapter is about you. Becoming a team coach is a journey rather than an event. It is important to continually build on your strengths and expertise through a process of reflection, practice and feedback, so that you can hone your skills and confidence. However busy you are, you need to set aside some time for your own personal reflection and development. Chapter 21 will help you to think about how to develop your skills and gain the support you need in the workplace to continue your own personal development.

10 common team challenges

Through our research and work with managers we have identified 10 common team challenges (see Figure 19.1). You may recognise some, or many, of these challenges from your own team experiences. These are issues which can handicap your team and prevent it from moving forward, but by working on them with the team you can help to build and improve performance. With each of the challenges, we have outlined how managers experience these situations and how you can use coaching to help to improve and work on the situation.

The coaching approaches we suggest often encompass an element of self-coaching, where you can reflect on how you are currently handling the situation and identify some options and ideas for moving forward. We also suggest ideas for one-to-one and team coaching where you can work towards a solution as a team.

Figure 19.1 10 common team challenges

The 10 common team challenges

1 Working across cultures

2 Personality clashes

3 Delegating

4 Lack of creativity

5 Dealing with poor performance

6 Leading teams through tough times

7 Moving from team member to team leader

8 Generational differences

9 Giving feedback

10 Managing upwards and outwards

However well your team is performing it's important to never be complacent; the best-performing teams understand that there is always room for improvement. You should never stop looking, revising and reviewing what you do and how you work together. One manager who has a high-performing team talked about his approach:

> The team I work with is highly engaged. Every quarter we have an external consultant to measure the engagement score. We currently have one of the best scores in the company, but my target is to improve this. My team is customer facing and it's important that they have the confidence to make decisions and develop new practices so we can keep our edge in the business. It's only by communicating, supporting each other and sharing ideas that we can do this, so team work is always at the top of my agenda.

Team challenges

TEAM CHALLENGE NO. 1: WORKING ACROSS CULTURES

Working with different cultures is fraught with problems. Whether you are working with different nationalities or different organisation and departmental cultures, the potential for misunderstandings and lack of awareness should not be underestimated. However, if you and the team can overcome these problems you have the opportunity for greater creativity and to innovate and perform at a higher level.

A key question is to ask yourself is whether the team is maximising the different working cultures within your team and externally. Your role as team leader is to coach and work with the team to bring out the richness and potential that working in a multicultural environment can bring.

How coaching can help

Step back and review the way the team is working. What do you notice?

- Are some people more dominant in meetings than others?
- Are there any challenges around language?
- Do people know each other?

- How do you adapt your approach?
- Are your meetings productive?

Make time for the team to get to know each other and build in some social time in meetings.

- Get team members from different cultures or organisations to share something about the way they work and have other team members ask questions to create greater understanding.
- Complete the team questionnaire together **(see page 78)** and discuss the results.
- Meet with your team on a one-to-one basis and understand more about how you can help and support them.
- Involve the team. Ask them to focus on a particular issue such as project review meetings, product development, customer service, etc. and consider how well you are working together. What else could be changed or improved to maximise the input from the different working cultures?
- One simple approach is to recognise and celebrate differences. A team leader we interviewed regularly holds 'National Day' events for different cultures and celebrates key festivals in the team meetings.
- Create opportunities for working with other team members from different cultures and locations. Match someone from your team for a period of time with someone in a team elsewhere. Then share this learning with the rest of the team.

TEAM CHALLENGE NO. 2: PERSONALITY CLASHES

When there is conflict in the team this has the potential to undermine team performance and morale, especially if the rest of the team spend time accommodating the clash. The rule for the team should be that whatever people think about each other personally, they must be able to put this to one side, to be professional and work together for the good of the team and, ultimately, for the good of the business. Whilst this is easier said than done, it's important to tackle any issue before it becomes a stumbling block for the whole team.

How coaching can help

Your role is very much to coach and work with the individuals involved. This can either be on a one-to-one basis, or together so that you can help facilitate a way forward:

- Understand what is going on. It is important to remain objective and not get pushed into taking sides.
- If you do feel compromised by the situation in any way, it may be useful to involve an external coach or arbitrator.
- Don't get pulled into the detailed content, but focus on helping them find a way through, so that you can all arrive at a solution everyone can buy into.
- Look for areas of common ground that both parties can agree on. If you can have a mutual purpose it's easier to identify what you need to do.
- Listen. The more you can allow others to talk, the more their emotions will subside and you can focus on a way forward together. However, remember to manage your time, summarise and move towards a solution.
- Finally, be clear about your expectations, explaining the impact on the team and, potentially, the wider organisation.
- Set up a review date where you can all review progress, acknowledge any changes and identify what else needs to happen to keep the relationships on track.

TEAM CHALLENGE NO. 3: DELEGATING

There are so many reasons why people don't delegate. It's important to understand what holds you back from delegating. Is it is fear of letting go, lack of trust, or concern that the team is already overloaded? It's worth questioning these reasons, as delegation can play a valuable role in increasing motivation and providing a valuable development opportunity for others. As one person we interviewed said: 'I could have done much more to empower others, if I had learned to delegate sooner. It would have helped me and the team.'

The key to success in delegation is in planning how you are going to delegate and combining it with coaching to maximise the development potential for the team. The first thing to do is to look at yourself and ask: what is stopping you delegating?

How coaching can help

- Look at your role. What elements can you delegate to help the team to grow and develop?

- Make sure you provide opportunities which combine autonomy, support and development.

- Look at delegation as a coaching opportunity, and link potential tasks to an individual's development need.

- Use more experienced team members to coach team members as they take on new roles and tasks.

- Make sure you provide good support so that people can develop at the pace that suits them. This is important: too fast and they may panic but if it all goes too slowly then they may feel patronised.

- Set up a delegation plan with team members where you can discuss the task, agree with them how to move ahead and build in feedback and review sessions.

- Review the delegation process on a regular basis so that you can understand how to hone and develop your approach.

TEAM CHALLENGE NO. 4: LACK OF CREATIVITY

If your team buzzes with creativity then you are truly blessed. Some teams struggle woefully to find creative ideas and for some sectors this is a crucial skill, making all the difference between success and failure. However, every team in any sector needs to factor creativity into its skillset.

How coaching can help

- Reflect on your own behaviour. Do you encourage creativity or just focus on the facts and details? Or do you like to come up with all the ideas yourself? Creativity is a team activity so make sure you involve everyone.

- Encourage people to look at things from a different perspective. One manager encouraged her team to pair up and visit a different environment such as an exhibition or art gallery to bring back new ideas. As she said: 'No one gets creative sitting at their desk all day'.

- Build creativity into your meetings. Brainstorm ideas together, break into groups to work on issues and take a 'walk and talk' to think about new approaches.
- Hold your meetings in different venues. It's important to get out of the everyday environment.
- Find the opportunity to network with people outside the organisation to bring back different perspectives and ideas.
- Invite speakers from different backgrounds and organisations.
- Reward and recognise new ideas which have been implemented.

TEAM CHALLENGE NO. 5: DEALING WITH POOR PERFORMANCE

Performance challenges are often difficult to tackle, but need to be dealt with before they become entrenched. For many managers there is a tendency to put off those difficult conversations, but the impact of this can have huge consequences not only in individual performance but on the performance and morale of the team. It can also affect the reputation of your team with other stakeholders. The key message is to deal with performance issues immediately; understand what is causing the issue and what can be done to help the person back on track.

How coaching can help

- Speak to the individual as soon as you see that performance is slipping. They may not recognise that there is a problem!
- Remember to keep the focus on the issue and behaviour which needs to change.
- Be clear and specific about your feedback and try to understand what is causing the problem. Often there are underlying issues which may be influencing the situation.
- Reflect back on times when this person has performed well and explore how you can get back to this level of performance again.
- Listen and ask questions to understand the situation before you jump in with solutions.
- Use the TOPIC model for coaching (see Chapter 3) to explore how you can move forward.

- Be supportive and encouraging, but also clear about your performance expectations.
- Set up regular review meetings so that you can monitor progress and provide feedback on improvements you are seeing. It's always worth making notes of these meetings and sharing them so you both know what is agreed.

TEAM CHALLENGE NO. 6: LEADING TEAMS THROUGH TOUGH TIMES

It's easy for teams to bond and work together when things are going well. However, when targets slip and pressures on the business increase it's not always that easy. Some people will thrive in this situation, but others will struggle.

Whilst working in a challenging environment can create opportunities to try new approaches and be more creative, it can also be a time of uncertainty for the team. As a team coach it's important to think about what you and the team can do to maintain your morale and motivation and to look for new ways to build your success.

How coaching can help

- Be aware of your own motivation and approach. If you are stressed, you will communicate this non-verbally through your behaviour. People will be quick to sense this and it may demotivate. Keeping a calm, positive persona will go a long way to maintaining morale.
- Be honest about the situation, and keep the team up to date on what is happening.
- Be aware of how individuals are coping with the situation and take time to talk and listen to people on an individual basis.
- Involve the team in working together to look at how to manage the situation and what they can do to help.
- Look for opportunities to develop new ideas, skills and approaches.
- Get creative and allow experimentation.
- Reward positive contributions and behaviour.

I took over a team that was underperforming and suffering from low morale. We had some tough targets to meet and were working in a very competitive environment.

The first, immediate change was that I sat with the team – I made sure I was visible and gave really clear feedback about what was happening in the business. People wanted to know the truth. The team lacked direction so we sat down as a team and came up with clear goals and objectives. This was followed up with half-hour chats with each team member to discuss 'what you can do' in the short, medium and long term to help us get there. We're now going to review against this in our next conversations. The fact that we were all focused on a clear goal and objective gave us something to organise around and everyone has a role to play in getting there.

TEAM CHALLENGE NO. 7: MOVING FROM TEAM MEMBER TO TEAM LEADER

Managing people who are colleagues, and even friends, is not always easy. The transition from being a team member to becoming the team manager can be challenging. You will need to reflect on what this means for your own behaviour and self-perception. What implications will this have for your relationship with colleagues? You also need to think about the type of team you want to create. This is your opportunity to shape the culture of the team and the way you work together. As Richard Reed, co-founder of Innocent Drinks points out:

Great businesses come from great teams. Surround yourself with a good team of people who have the same values as you, but with different skills.

How coaching can help

- Take time to reflect on what the new role means for you. What old behaviours and approaches will you have to leave behind and what new behaviours will you have to adopt?
- It's often useful to get some external coaching support or mentoring when you are moving through a career transition. Having a sounding

board can help you think through how you want to shape and develop your leadership approach.

- Recognise what will stay the same in the way you work with your team and what will need to change. You may need to set up some new processes and ways of working to support this.

- Set up a team event which you organise and lead to establish your role and involve the team in thinking about how you work together.

- Be clear about the culture you want to achieve in the team, set objectives and tackle any performance issues immediately.

- Remember, any change takes a bit of time to work through, so appreciate that this may not be easy for others and take the time to talk to the team and see how they are feeling.

Insight

As one team leader shared:

I recently stepped up into a new role in which my old colleagues became my reports and, needless to say, this came with challenges. I recognised that I needed to have some difficult conversations to resolve an awkward situation with a colleague. It wasn't easy but now it's one of the best relationships I have in the organisation.

TEAM CHALLENGE NO. 8: GENERATIONAL DIFFERENCES

Increasingly now teams are becoming more multigenerational. A mix of generations can bring with it a combination of experience, wisdom, creativity and fresh ideas. However, it can also create challenges as the younger members of the workforce, often referred to as Generation Ys (those born between 1980 and 2000), have a different perspective on the workplace. Research points to the fact that Generation Ys thrive on feedback and are hungry for career progression. They can also get frustrated with some of their older, less tech savvy, colleagues. Equally, the older generations, often referred to as the 'baby boomers', have grown up in a different environment. But don't assume that they are winding down: many want to take on new roles and are keen to continue their development.

How coaching can help

- Think about the make-up of your team and reflect on how the generational mix is working.

- Help team members appreciate the strengths they bring as individuals.

- Set up projects and tasks with a mix of people so you can maximise the potential in the team.

- If there are any areas of frustration, discuss them as a team and individually, so you can work out ways of working together effectively.

- Make sure you provide adequate training and personal development plans for all team members.

- Think about setting up mentoring relationships. Some organisations have complemented the traditional mentoring approach by providing 'upwards mentoring' where younger employees can mentor others in the use of technology or thinking about the customer base from a different perspective.

- Provide regular feedback to team members and adapt this to their needs and preferences.

TEAM CHALLENGE NO. 9: GIVING FEEDBACK

Feedback given and received well, in a timely manner, can help performance to flourish and allow people to achieve their potential. However, done badly it can cause de-motivation, ill feeling and loss of confidence. Equally, when people receive no feedback at all this can be disconcerting and discouraging.

Your challenge as a team coach is to create the right balance of feedback for your team members and deliver it in a way that is perceived as helpful and developmental.

How coaching can help

- Refer back to the SOFA model (page 30). This is a useful tool to plan for any feedback you want to give your team.

- Remember to keep a balance in your feedback. Don't just focus on the improvement areas but look at the positives and how you can build on them.

- Don't assume that if people are performing 'they are just doing what's expected' so don't need feedback. Knowing they are doing well and encouraging them to continue can make a big difference to increasing overall motivation.
- Give feedback immediately, don't save it up as it won't have as much value and impact.
- Feedback and coaching go hand in hand. Use coaching to look at ways of working with the feedback to build performance.
- Remember that feedback is a two-way process. Ask people to assess their own performance. Get their views on what they do well and how they could improve.
- Encourage a feedback culture in your team, and also seek feedback from the team so you can improve your performance as well.

TEAM CHALLENGE NO. 10: MANAGING UPWARDS AND OUTWARDS

Teams don't operate in isolation. Their success relies on effectively managing the context and environment in which they work. This means working effectively with other teams and departments internally and also relating to any external customers, partners and suppliers. It also requires you and the team to manage upwards with your own boss and others who may be impacted by how your team operates.

How coaching can help

Reflect on how much time you spend on this. It is an important aspect of your role, which will help you to support and safeguard your team:

- Do you have a good network in the organisation and with your external stakeholders?
- Are you aware of who these stakeholders are?
- How effective are you at working with and responding to your boss?

These are all important personal questions and if you are struggling with answering them it may be worth thinking about working with a mentor or external coach to identify how you can develop this aspect of your role.

Other approaches you can take with your team are:

- Develop a stakeholder map together to identify your key stakeholders.
- Share the responsibility in the team for managing these relationships and building on the internal networks of your team members.
- Look at where there are gaps and make sure someone is responsible for filling them.
- Spend time understanding your stakeholders. Listen to their views, look for areas of common ground and find out how you can work together more effectively.
- Involve your stakeholders in changes you are proposing in the team as you will need their buy-in and support.
- Regularly review your progress and identify potential problem areas before they become an issue.

Our definition of team coaching is:

Engaging in a shared purpose that is focused on improving performance and developing individual and team capabilities to achieve game-changing results.

All the ideas and suggestions we have made are ones which will involve you in reflecting on your own approach and coaching the team to build on and develop their skills and expertise.

Frequently asked questions (FAQs)

Whether or not people have experience of coaching, they often have questions about the practical issues around their coaching skills and approach and what to do in different situations. We have picked some of the most frequently asked questions so you have a quick coaching reference guide to help you build your skills.

I DON'T HAVE TIME TO COACH, WHAT CAN I DO?

Having time to coach shouldn't be an issue if you build it into your overall leadership approach. By asking good, open questions and using the TOPIC approach (see Chapter 3), the chances are that your conversations will become more focused and that problem-solving can be shared with the team. Coaching and delegation also go hand in hand so if you want to delegate, use a coaching approach to build capability and confidence and this will help with your overall time management.

PEOPLE IN THE TEAM ARE RESISTANT TO THE IDEA OF COACHING – WHAT SHOULD I DO?

You need to explore the reasons behind this view. Sometimes this reluctance can be a misperception. Some people mistakenly believe that coaching is a remedial process, only used when someone is performing badly. Start slowly, and gradually change your approach by asking questions and encouraging people to develop ideas. You don't even need to mention the word coaching if you think it will cause concerns.

CAN I GIVE ADVICE?

It's always best to explore to all the possible options, and ask the others about their thoughts and ideas before making suggestions. In some cases where there is a really clear answer it would be frustrating and unhelpful for the other person if you didn't advise them. However, beware of doing this too much, and too often because:

- if you are always giving advice, people won't make decisions but will come to you.
- your advice may not be the only perspective and may not be correct.
- as a coach your role is to help others develop their thinking and come up with ideas.
- generally, people are more committed if they come up with their own solutions.

WHY DO I FEEL UNCOMFORTABLE IF I DON'T HAVE AN ANSWER?

This is a feeling you need to let go of. It really is impossible to have answers for all the situations we face. Coaching and involving others in coming up with solutions is a real leadership skill which will build creativity and connection in the team. Your role is to facilitate and coach the team to come up with the best possible way forward.

WHAT DO I DO WHEN COACHING DOESN'T WORK?

If you are feeling that your coaching approach isn't working, the best way to understand this is to ask why. Professional coaches go through a contracting process with the people they are coaching, where they agree how they are going to work together. They review how this is working on a regular basis.

You may need to be more explicit about the contracting and what you are trying to achieve. Alternatively, explain more about why you are taking a coaching approach, and explore why it isn't working. By discussing the issue you will both be able to come up with ideas to help you adapt the process.

I HAVE SOMEONE OLDER THAN ME IN THE TEAM – HOW DO I COACH THEM?

Age shouldn't be an issue in coaching as it's about respecting the individual and their ideas and views. It's about understanding other people's points of view, exploring, challenging and supporting their thinking. Check out your assumptions about the other person. Is this more of an issue for you than them? If you take age out of the equation, what is the real challenge in this coaching relationship? How can you use a coaching approach to understand more about this?

WHEN DO I GET A PROFESSIONAL COACH INVOLVED?

Working with a professional coach can be valuable for your team. As well as their skills and expertise, a professional coach will bring an outside perspective and will see the team with fresh eyes. They also have a more neutral perspective and can reflect back what they are seeing and experiencing and help the team to develop. However, as a team leader you are the constant element in the team and it's important to work with the coach to develop your skills and confidence so that team coaching can be a central element of your leadership repertoire.

I NOTICE THAT WHILST THE TEAM ARE RESPONDING WELL TO MY COACHING APPROACH THEY ARE RELUCTANT TO COACH EACH OTHER – WHAT CAN I DO?

It may be that the team is unaware of how to coach each other and what coaching is. Perhaps you could arrange some training, or share some of the ideas and approaches in this book. Discuss how the team could benefit from taking more of a coaching approach in the way they work. You could also set up some coaching pairs, with more experienced people coaching some of the newer team members.

HOW SHOULD I RESPOND TO MY BOSS? THEY THINK COACHING IS SOMETHING THAT ONLY WEAK TEAMS NEED AND DON'T APPRECIATE WHAT I AM TRYING TO DO

You may need to explain what you are trying to achieve with your team and how you are going about it. Finding a quick win that will demonstrate to your boss the value of coaching may help to change their viewpoint. This may be a new idea the team developed, or an example of the team supporting and coaching each other to achieve a target.

If you and the team are taking a coaching approach it should also be evident in the way you work as a team and the level of motivation and morale in the team.

I DON'T FEEL I HAVE THE RIGHT SKILLS TO BE A COACH – WHAT CAN I DO ABOUT THIS?

At its simplest level coaching is about developing and bringing out the potential in others. If you hold this at the front of your mind, the chances are you will be practising and using many of the skills and techniques of a good coach. Review your progress on a weekly basis and think about what you have done to coach and develop others. Refer back to Part one of this book to refresh your knowledge. Coaching is something which needs practice, and gradually it will become part of your everyday leadership approach.

HOW DO I START TO COACH THE TEAM?

You can start coaching immediately. The first thing you need to do is build coaching into your everyday conversations, making it part of your overall leadership approach. Listen and ask questions rather than jumping to solutions, and encourage people to come up with ideas. It's also a good idea to think about the development needs in your team and how you can help the team to progress and grow. As a team coach you need to think about the individuals in the team and the team as whole, so take time to review how the team is working together and then use some of the ideas from the book in your team meetings.

Getting support and developing your skills

Coaching and leading a team is not an easy task and it is well worth thinking about the support and development you need in your role. Professional coaches have what is known as supervision. They will work with another coach or group of coaches to help them improve their coaching practice. This also provides the opportunity to discuss some of the challenges they face and to reflect on how to move ahead. In addition, most professional coaches will make sure that each year they update their skills and knowledge in some way. There are a number of support mechanisms you can use as shown in Figure 21.1.

Figure 21.1 Support mechanisms to help you develop as a team coach

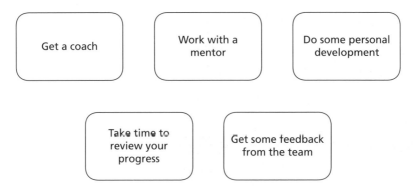

GET A COACH

The coach needs a coach! Professional coaching can provide you with a great sounding board to develop your team coaching approach. It will give you the opportunity to review your progress, and reflect on new ways of working.

WORK WITH A MENTOR

A mentor, either within or outside the organisation, can provide you with advice, guidance and expertise on many of the challenges you may be experiencing. Just to remind you, a mentor is usually someone who is more experienced and able to offer guidance.

DO SOME PERSONAL DEVELOPMENT

Working on your own personal development is very important, whether this is attending a workshop or training event, reading a relevant book or article, or getting feedback from others. Try to set aside some time each month for your own development, after all you can't expect your team to develop if you don't do the same.

GET SOME FEEDBACK FROM THE TEAM

Ask your team for some feedback on your approach:

- What do they think you are doing well?
- What would they like more of?
- What should you do differently?

TAKE TIME TO REVIEW YOUR PROGRESS

One important way of continuing to develop is to review your progress each month:

- What has gone well?
- What new things have you tried and how effective were they?
- What feedback have you received from others?
- What would you like to improve on?
- What would you like to do differently next month?

Set aside an hour each month to review your progress and reflect on any changes you may want to make.

Insight

Here is an example of how one manager we worked with reviewed her progress:

> The demands on my team were changing. We were being asked to move from being a central processing unit to providing a relationship and service to the different business units. This was not easy as it meant that the team had to reorganise and take on new ways of working. I found the best way to keep track of how the team was moving ahead was to keep some notes on how we were progressing.

▶

CURRENT SITUATION	ACTIONS	REFLECTIONS	NEXT STEPS
We needed to change the way the team operated.	• We held two team meetings to explain and think about how to move ahead as a team. • We used the first meeting to focus on what we needed to do – our purpose and objectives – and the second session to reflect on the skills, roles and responsibilities.	• Whilst we have come up with some good ideas and a training schedule, some team members are finding it difficult to adapt to the change. • We also seem to be slipping back into our old habits of focusing on financial detail at the expense of business support.	• Individual coaching sessions to support the team and set some objectives and development. • I am using some of the enthusiastic team members to coach and support others. • Team progress review meeting to reflect on progress and customer feedback. • I have also set up a mentoring relationship to bounce off ideas.

TAKE AWAY

Review your progress regularly. Work with the team and use your coaching approach to involve others and stay on track.

Use the template below to review your progress with coaching your team.

CURRENT SITUATION	ACTIONS	REFLECTIONS	NEXT STEPS

Top tips

Suggestions for maintaining a great coaching relationship

Coaching is a two-way process, and great coaching requires the commitment, involvement and curiosity from both the person or team being coached and the coach. It is not something you do to others but something you do together, and through the process new ideas and options can be explored.

Here are some tips to help you and your team get the most out of any coaching relationship. They may be worth sharing with your team so they understand more about the overall approach.

Tips for the team coach:

- Always have an open mind and listen to what others are saying.
- Don't shut down ideas: be curious and ask questions to explore ideas and options.
- Be patient and don't lose sight of the objective of the coaching session.
- Build an individual coaching relationship with each team member.
- Work with the strengths in the team and try to build in opportunities for team members to develop and grow.
- Encourage involvement from all team members.
- Be aware of the energy in the team and how you are feeling and reacting. Reflect this back and use it to help the team to develop the way they work together.
- Create and encourage coaching relationships to develop between all team members.

Tips for team members:

- Be curious and recognise that there are different solutions and ideas to most situations.
- Listen to others and ask questions to find out about their ideas and concerns.

▶

- Don't get stuck in the problem: focus on developing solutions and moving forward.
- Try to provide an environment of support and challenge in the team and be aware of what you bring to the team.
- Build your own self-awareness, and awareness of others, so that you can appreciate different approaches and recognise the strengths in others.

When you build a coaching environment in your team it means that everyone is responsible for the solution.

Conclusion: Achieving game-changing results

We hope that we have given you plenty of food for thought and plenty of suggestions and ideas to improve the way you work with your team.

There are three key points that will help you apply the learning from this book:

1 Involve everyone in the team in the process of building a coaching culture with clear parameters. Help them to see how they fit into the big picture of team success. If you have a team where people only know about what they do then this is unlikely to be a high-performing team.

2 Keep developing your skills and understand that as a team coach you have to build confidence, competence and commitment in the team. You should be the biggest fan of your team!

3 Identify what the game-changers are for the business and make sure that as a team coach you develop the skills and potential of the team to meet the needs of the organisation.

We hope that this book has provided you with plenty of ideas and tips for you and your team, so that you can grow and develop together. High-performing teams have a real *can-do* approach, generating enthusiasm, energy and achieving excellent results. Your role as a team coach is at the heart of this success.

We wish you and your team well on your journey.

References

Introduction

1. Woods, M. and Welyne, T., 2002. Personal Leadership Development Study. Business Wire.

2. Sorenson, S., 2013. *How employee engagement drives growth.* [online] Gallup. Available at: **<www.gallup.com/businessjournal/163130/employee-engagement-drives-growth.aspx>**

3. Whitmore, J., 2009. *Coaching for performance.* London: Nicholas Brearley.

4. Hicks, J. and Townsend, N.W., 2002. *The U.S. Army War College: military education in a democracy.* Philadelphia, PA: Temple University Press.

Chapter 1

1. Goleman, D., Boyatzis, R., and Hay Group. *The Emotional and Social Competency Inventory Workbook.* Hay Group. Available at: www.haygroup.com/leadershipan dtalentondemand/ourproducts/item_details.aspx?itemid=58&type=1&t=2>

2. Brewerton, P. and Brook, J., 2010. *Strengths for success: your pathway to peak performance.* London: Strength Partnership Press.

Chapter 2

1. Wheatley, M.J., 2009. *Turning to one another: simple conversations to restore hope to the future.* San Francisco, CA: Berrett-Koehler Publishers, Inc.

2. O'Connor, J. and McDermott, I., 2013. *Principles of NLP: the only introduction you'll ever need.* London: Thorsons.

3. Frederickson, B., 2009. *Positivity.* New York, NY: Crown Publishers.

Chapter 3

1. Rackham, N. and Carlisle, J., 1978. The effective negotiator. *Journal of European Industrial Training,* 2(7), p.2–5.

Chapter 4

1. Belbin, R.M., 2010. *Team roles at work.* Oxford: Taylor & Francis.

Chapter 5

1. Katzenbach, J.R. and Smith, D.K., 2006. *The wisdom of teams.* New York, NY: Collins Business Essentials.
2. Tuckman, B., 1965. Developmental sequence in small groups. *Psychological Bulletin,* 63(6), pp. 384–99.

Chapter 6

1. Janis, I.L., 1972. *Victims of groupthink: a psychological study of foreign-policy decisions and fiascoes.* Boston, MA: Houghton, Mifflin.

Chapter 7

1. Baghai, M., Coley, S. and White, D., 2000. *The alchemy of growth*: practical insights for building the enduring enterprise. London: Perseus Books.

Chapter 8

1. Kaplan, Inc., 2014. *Enhancing performance management: the value of staff appraisals.* [pdf] *Kaplan, Inc.* Available at: <**http://kaplan.co.uk/docs/default-source/pdfs/kaplan_b2b_appraisal_report.pdf?sfvrsn=2**>
2. Holton, V., Dent, F. and Rabbetts, J., 2008. *Ashridge Management Index 2008: meeting the challenges of the 21st century.* [pdf]. *Ashridge.* Available at: <**https://www.ashridge.org.uk/Media-Library/Ashridge/PDFs/Publications/MeetingTheChallengesOfThe21stCentury.pdf**>
3. Trenier, E., 2013. Maximising performance through strengths: an illustration of strengths-based performance management. *Assessment & Development Matters,* 5(1), pp.13–15.

4. Buckingham, M. and Goodall, A., 2015. Reinventing performance management. *HBR,* April.

5. Stanleigh, M., 2015. *New directions in performance management.* [online] Business Improvement Architects. Available at: **<https://bia.ca/ new-directions-for-performance-management/>**

6. Block, L., 2015. *Work rules!: insights from inside Google that will transform how you live and lead.* London: John Murray.

Chapter 9

1. Pentland, A.S., 2012. The new science of building great teams. *HBR,* April.

Chapter 10

1. Kübler-Ross, E., 1969. *On death and dying: what the dying have to teach doctors, nurses, clergy & their own families.* New York, NY: Scribner.

Chapter 11

1. *Ashridge Management Index 2008: meeting the challenges of the 21st century.* [pdf]. *Ashridge.* Available at: **<https://www. ashridge.org.uk/Media-Library/Ashridge/PDFs/Publications/ MeetingTheChallengesOfThe21stCentury.pdf>**

2. George, M., 2013. 5 steps to creating employee engagement. [online] *Appirio.* Available at: **<http://appirio.com/category/business-blog/ it/2013/07/5-steps-to-creating-employee-engagement/>**

3. Adkins, A., 2015. Only 35% of U.S. managers are engaged in their jobs. [online] *Gallup.* Business Journal, April 2. Available at: **<www.gallup.com/ businessjournal/182228/managers-engaged-jobs.aspx>**

4. Buckingham, M. and Coffman, C., 1999. *First break all the rules: what the world's greatest managers do differently.* London: Simon & Schuster.

Chapter 12

1. Stress Management Society, 2015. Practical help to ease stress in the workplace. [online] Available at: <**www.stress.org.uk/ workplace-wellbeing-solutions**>

2. **www.personalstrengthsuk.com**, OPP, 2015. [online] Available at: <**www.opp.co.uk**>

3. National Business Research Institute, 2015. A culture of levity at work. [pdf] Available at: <**www.nbrii.com/employee-survey-white-papers/ a-culture-of-levity-at-work/**>

4. Chartered Institute of Personnel and Development, 2006. *Annual survey report 2006: how engaged are British employees?* [pdf] *CIPD.*

5. Headspace, 2015. [online] Available at: <**www.headspace.com**>

Chapter 13

1. Lencioni, P.M., 2002. *The five dysfunctions of a team: a leadership fable.* San Francisco, CA: Jossey-Bass.

2. Economist Intelligence Unit, 2008. *The role of trust in business collaboration.* [pdf] Economist Intelligence Unit. Available at: <**http://graphics.eiu.com/ upload/cisco_trust.pdf**>

3. West, T., 2013. *The challenge of leading: insights from the Clipper Round the World Yacht Race.* [pdf] Ashridge Executive Education. Available at: <**www.ashridge.org.uk/getattachment/Faculty-Research/Research/Current-Research/Research-Projects/Clipper-Research/Clipper-Report_Executive-Summary.pdf**>

Chapter 14

1. McKinsey & Company, 2015. *Building capabilities for performance.* [online] McKinsey & Company. Available at: <**www.mckinsey.com/ business-functions/organization/our-insights/building-capabilities-for-performance**>

2. Corporate Research Forum, 2015. *Leadership development: is it fit for purpose?* [online] CRF. Available at: **<www.crforum.co.uk/research-and-resources/leadership-development-is-it-for-for-purpose/>**

3. Waller, L., 2011. *From the classroom to the workplace: Ensuring the transfer of learning.* [pdf] Ashridge Executive Education.

Chapter 15

1. Rogers, C.R., 2004. *On becoming a person: a therapist's view of psychotherapy.* London: Constable & Robinson.

2. Personal Strengths Publishing, 2015. *Strength deployment inventory.* [online] Available at: **<www.personalstrengths.com>**

3. Thomas, K.W. and Kilmann, R., 2002. *The Thomas Kilmann Conflict Mode Instrument.* [online] Kilmann Diagnostics. Available at: **<www.kilmanndiagnostics.com/overview-thomas-kilmann-conflict-mode-instrument-tki>**

Chapter 16

1. Lavine, L., 2014. How to reclaim thousands of wasted hours each year. [online] Fast Company. Available at: **<http://www.fastcompany.com/3030352/work-smart/how-to-reclaim-thousands-of-wasted-hours-each-year>**

2. Atlassian. You waste a lot of time at work. [online] Available at: **<https://www.atlassian.com/time-wasting-at-work-infographic** [online infographic]

3. Bluedorn, A.C., Turban, D.B., Love, M.S., 1999. The effects of stand-up and sit-down meeting formats on meeting outcomes. *Journal of Applied Psychology*, 84(2), 277–285.

Chapter 17

1. Siebdrat, F., Hoegl, M., Holger, E., 2009. *How to manage virtual teams.* [online] MIT Sloan Management Review, July. Available at: **<http://sloanreview.mit.edu/article/how-to-manage-virtual-teams/>**

2. Unify, 2014. *Unify New Way to Work Index: the habits of successful virtual teams.* [pdf] Unify. Available at: **<http://www.unify.com/tr/~/media/ internet-2012/documents/nw2w/Survey-Report_2.pdf>**

3. Lepsinger, R., 2010. *Virtual team failure: six common reasons why virtual teams do not succeed.* [online] Business Know-How. Available at: **<www. businessknowhow.com/manage/virtualteam.htm>**

4. The Economist Intelligence Unit, 2009. *Managing virtual teams: taking a more strategic approach.* [online] The Economist Intelligence Unit. Available at: **<www.economistinsights.com/business-strategy/analysis/ managing-virtual-teams/fullreport>**

5. Siebdrat, F., Hoegl, M., Holgar, E., 2009. *How to manage virtual teams.* [online] MIT Sloan Management Review, July. Available at: **<http:// sloanreview.mit.edu/article/how-to-manage-virtual-teams/>**

6. Siemens Enterprise Communications, 2012. *The untapped potential of virtual teams.* [online] Siemens Enterprise Communications. Available at: **<http://resources.idgenterprise.com/original/AST-0087742_The_Untapped_ Potential_of_Virtual_Teams.pdf>**

7. Ashridge, 2005. Cultural working preference tool.

8. Jarvenpaa L., Leidner D., 1999. Communication and trust in global virtual teams. *Organization Science,* 10(6), pp.777 – 790.

Chapter 18

1   Jones, P., Holton, V., 2006. *Teams – succeeding in complexity.* Berkhamsted: Ashridge.

2. Wasserman, T., 2012. *Email takes up 28% of workers' time.* [online] MashableUK. Available at: **<http://mashable.com/2012/08/01/ email-workers-time/>**

3. Briggs Myers, I. and Myers, P.B., 1995. *Gifts differing: understanding personality type.* Mountain View, CA: Davies-Black Publishing.

Recommended resources

Books

Newton, R., 2014. *Managing your team through change.* Harlow: Pearson Education.

Whitmore, J., 2009. *Coaching for performance: GROWing human potential and purpose – the principles and practice of coaching and leadership.* London: Nicholas Brealey.

Meyer, E., 2014. *The culture map: breaking through the invisible boundaries of global business.* New York, NY: PublicAffairs.

Jones, P., 2014. *The performance management pocketbook.* Alresford: Management Pocketbooks.

Jackson, P.Z. and McKergow, M., 2007. *The solutions focus: making coaching and change simple.* London: Nicholas Brealey.

Hayes, P., 2011. *Leading and coaching teams to success: the secret life of teams.* Maidenhead: Open University Press McGraw Hill Education.

McGee, P., 2013. *How to succeed with people.* Chichester: Capstone Press.

Harvard Business School, 2013. *HBR's 10 must reads on teams,* Boston, MA: Harvard Business School Publishing.

Hawkins, P., 2014. *Leadership team coaching: developing collective transformational leadership.* London: Kogan Page.

Other useful resources

Belbin: **www.belbin.com**

Strength Deployment Inventory (SDI): **www.personalstrengths.com**

Thomas-Kilmann Instrument: **www.kilmanndiagnostics.com**

Mind Tools: **www.mindtools.com**

TED Talks: **www.ted.com**

Index

Facebook 126
face-to-face meetings 218, 233–4
facilitation
    of effective meetings 219
    leadership approach for 7–9
    skills 32–7, *33f*, 39–43
feedback
    as development tool 185–6
    for measuring success of meetings
        215–17
    as support for team coach 274
    as team challenge 264–5
    as team coaching skill 29–30, *29f*
First break all the rules (Buckingham
    and Coffman) 152
five Ps of performance and potential
    180–1, *180f*, 190–1
force field analysis 134–5, *135f*
formal development programmes 189
forming stage of team development
    68–9
forums, for building collaboration
    126
four game-changing aspects of team
    communication *198f*
four Rs of successful performance
    management 109–10, *109f*
frequently asked questions
    267–71
future focus 101–2, *100f*

Gallup 21, 152
game-changing results, achieving
    xix–xx, 278
Generations Ys 263
goals
    building alignment of 108–9,
        109f
    criteria for 109–10
    setting the 99–102
    understanding of team 94–6, *95f*
Google 115, 220
ground rules for team working
    86–7
group dynamics in team meetings
    219
'groupthink' 87

hangout meetings 220
Hay Group 9
Head, Heart and Gut model
    in design of team meetings 214–15
    preferences for motivation 149–51
    preferred communication styles
        245–6
    for team analysis 45–52, *46–9t, 50f,
        50t, 51f*
healthy lifestyles, for building
    resilience 163

ideas exchange, for building
    collaboration 126
impact, for successful virtual teams
    235
individual coaching, difference
    between team and xiii–xiv
information technology, for building
    collaboration 126
introversion, and preferred
    communication styles 246
involvement of team
    for building engagement 153–4
    for meetings 219–21
    for meetings design 217–19
issue, aspect of conversation 200–2

key performance indicators, and
    emotions at work 162, *162f*
knowledge, failure to capture 225

language barriers 225, 233
leadership approach
    assessing own 5–9
    changing views of xvii
    coaching in everyday 253, 271
    for successful virtual teams
        234–6
    and trust 172–3
levity, for building resilience 162, 163
listening
    for building resilience 163
    for emotions 23–5, *23f*, 258
    for successful virtual teams 231
    as team coaching skill 22–5
location, of team meeting 220

time, lack of for coaching 267
TOPIC model of team coaching
40–2, *41f*
tough times, as team challenge 261–2
trust 168–78, *170f, 177f*
Tuckman, Bruce 68
Tuckman team stages model 68–9, *68f*

unconditional positive regard 204
understanding
    building for trust 174–5
    stakeholders *138f*
    of team 44–5, *45f*, 60, 83–6
U-SHAPER model for team
    performance 76

VACE characteristics of good
    collaboration 120–1
value, demonstrating 270
virtual teams 223–4, 236
    communication challenges 224–5
    communication process 226–8
    leadership approach for successful
        234–6
    successful and unsuccessful 226
    task, relationships and team
        performance *226f*
    ways of improving effectiveness
        228–34

virtual working 223–4
VUCA (volatility, uncertainty,
        complexity and ambiguity)
        world xv
VW (Volkswagen) cars 87

'walk and talk,' for problem-solving
        220
ways of working (WOWs)
    developing successful *228f*
    for successful virtual teams 229
weaknesses, in SWOT
        analysis 84–5
WEE (words, emotions, energy)
        model for effective listening
        23, *23f*
Whitmore, John xiii
working together
    for building trust 175–6
    lack of 225
    when coach and team
        not 269
work-life balance, for building
        resilience 164
workload control, for building
        resilience 164
'world café' meetings 221

yes AND, rather than yes BUT 220